found art

found art

discovering beauty in foreign places

leeana tankersley

ZONDERVAN®

ZONDERVAN.com/
AUTHORTRACKER
follow your favorite authors

ZONDERVAN

Found Art
Copyright © 2009 by Leeana Miller Tankersley

This title is also available in a Zondervan audio edition.
Visit www.zondervan.fm.

Requests for information should be addressed to:
Zondervan, *Grand Rapids, Michigan 49530*

Library of Congress Cataloging-in-Publication Data

Tankersley, Leeana, 1975-
      Found art : discovering beauty in foreign places / Leeana Tankersley.
            p.   cm.
      ISBN 978-0-310-29133-6 (hardcover)
      1. Spirituality — Meditations. I. Title.
      BL624.2.T36   2009
      270.8'3082 — dc22   2009021154

Interior design by Beth Shagene

Printed in the United States of America

09 10 11 12 13 14 • 23 22 21 20 19 18 17 16 15 14 13 12 11 10 9 8 7 6 5 4 3 2 1

To all those who have kept vigils for me.
Especially Steve.

contents

a swatch of black silk from a borrowed *abaya*

a mesquite leaf

a navy seal trident

a receipt from the russian-georgian restaurant on louisiana street

There is a time for everything,
and a season for every activity under the heavens:

a time to be born and a time to die,
a time to plant and a time to uproot,

a time to kill and a time to heal,
a time to break down and a time to build up,

a time to weep and a time to laugh,
a time to mourn and a time to dance,

a time to scatter stones and a time to gather them,
a time to embrace and a time to turn away,

a time to search and a time to quit searching,
a time to hold on and a time to let go,

a time to tear and a time to mend,
a time to be silent and a time to speak,

a time to love and a time to hate,
a time for war and a time for peace. . . .

He has made everything beautiful in its time.

He has also set eternity in the human heart;
yet no one can fathom what God has done
from beginning to end.

Ecclesiastes 3:1–8, 11

my collage

an introduction

At twenty-seven, I married the love of my life and moved to the Middle East. One year later, we returned to the States, changed. This is the story of that journey, the literal journey of living in a foreign culture, of exploring and experiencing a place so incredibly new to me that most of what I knew about myself and the world to that point would be challenged in some way.

While the story is literal, it is also figurative. As you may well know, foreign territory doesn't only exist ten thousand miles away; we can find ourselves in unknown countries without going anywhere.

Like healing, for instance. Healing can be one of the most foreign things we do if we've never been taught how or shown that one could survive the pursuit and process of becoming whole. Grief is similar. If we've never seen how to grieve or never been allowed to or never given ourselves the permission to mourn a deep loss, then grief is foreign to us.

More often than not, we are refugees, working through the seasons of life with foreign soil under our nails, never sure exactly where we belong or how we will manage. We rarely know the language, culture, or climate, and we often have little sense of where God is in our displacement.

For years, I have found solace in the third chapter of the Old Testament book Ecclesiastes. Without its truth, I am sure life would make much less sense to me, especially the spirituality of life.

I believe the author of Ecclesiastes to be right-on with his assessment of our days here on earth: There is a time for everything, a season for every activity under heaven. A time to be born and a time to die, a time to plant and a time to uproot, a time to kill and a time to heal, and so on.

We can count on experiencing breakneck joys as well as abysmal defeats. And in spite of all the ups and downs, God is making everything beautiful in its time. The grim stickiness, the author of Ecclesiastes points out, is that we don't always know what God is doing from beginning to end.

I am one of those people who spends much of life agitated and scared and drinking far too much Diet Coke because I typically don't know what God is up to. When I read that he just might be making some beauty out of *my* life, well, that is exceedingly good news. I don't know about you, but that's the kind of news I can really use right now, seeing as how the world feels sideways at least half the time.

My life is wildly all over the place, a collection of all kinds of strange raw material that often makes little sense to me in the moment. The war grieves me. Financial woes keep me up at night. Shame haunts me. Fear keeps me company pretty much around the clock. But what if God were taking all of my life — the glorious and the gutless, the griefs and the gains — and piecing each bit together like a collage so that when finished, something extraordinary would emerge?

If the author of Ecclesiastes is right, as I believe he is, then God is at work even now, creating and recreating an enduring piece of art from my little old, broken-down, Diet Coke-saturated life. That is what we call *found art*—a genre of art that started umpteen years ago with a guy in New York who took a urinal and cleverly refashioned it into a fountain. Found art is created when odd, disparate, unlikely, even long-abandoned castoffs are put together with other similarly unexpected remnants to create something new and, if all goes as planned, lovely.

Because such art is essentially redemptive, found art is also deeply spiritual, predating even urinal-man in its origins. In God's hands, spit and mud become sight. Dust and rib become humanity. Darkness and void become world. Fishermen become followers. Virgin becomes mother. Water becomes wine. Empty nets become overflowing. Death is somehow miraculously refashioned into life.

When I arrived in the Middle East, I realized I was looking at a half-me, a fragmented soul walking around town. I had given away pieces of myself, convinced the giving had all been for good causes. During this journey, I discovered it was high time I felt the losses, collected the pieces, and reclaimed myself.

That's the thing about these journeys into foreign places. They have a way of making us different if we will let them. We can resist the beauty that is waiting for us, but if we will enter the frightening place—if we will engage ourselves in the context of this new culture—we will see that there was no shortcut to transformation.

Life is most certainly a collage of experience, with all the scraps and secondhand oddments overlaying one another. On a few special occasions we are able to glimpse the art-in-the-making—the found art—that is created from these throwaway bits.

To that end, I invite you to look at this entire book as a collage of sorts:

- a handwritten note from Kuwait
- a braid of fringe from a Persian rug
- an original poem
- a bit of basting thread
- a swatch of black silk from a borrowed *abaya*
- a mesquite leaf
- a Navy SEAL Trident
- a receipt from the Russian-Georgian restaurant on Louisiana Street

Each of these items would be glued down, taped on, and pinned together—snippets and remnants that, in time, have collectively become something beautiful.

As you read my collage, I will be breathing a prayer for you. My prayer is that you will enter the foreign territories, and in them your own art will be found.

Leeana Tankersley

found art

a handwritten note from kuwait

1
uprooting

Somebody unplug the hair dryer, I thought to myself as I stepped out of Bahrain International Airport and into the hot night. Part suffocating humidity and part dry desert wind, the air was vaguely reminiscent of a July I spent in Hattiesburg, Mississippi, visiting my older sister, Laura, and her husband.

In Mississippi, the air was Southern-accent thick, and her prewar, non-air-conditioned house groaned from the sticky heat. Every day I would try in vain to dry my hair—the heat from the dryer mixing with the incessant humidity. That's exactly what the Bahrain air felt like—dry and wet all at the same time, intolerable as a hair dryer in Hattiesburg.

Similar in feel, but very different in smell. No hint of forthcoming rain or the pungency of fresh-cut grass or the sweat of magnolia trees. The scent was far rawer, certainly different from my hometown San Diego air I had left just thirty-six hours ago with its polite and accommodating ocean breezes. Cigarette smoke, incense-infused musk barely masking sour body odor, and curry all rode the hot wind into my nose, chased by twinges of Gulf water and gasoline.

I was standing in the middle of a new world. In the words of Aldous Huxley, Bahrain would become a "brave new world" with time. In that first introductory moment, though, everything was just new. The heat, the air, and the smells were all right at home, but clearly I was not. I believe the word is *foreign*. I'm not sure if Bahrain was more foreign to me or I was more foreign to it. We were a strange pair, to be sure.

While the scene outside the terminal was a common one, it felt anything but that to me. White ankle-length *thobes* paced the sidewalk, followed by ground-kissing black *abayas* floating ethereally as though there were no feet under them — a graceful and yet hollow effect I was instantly intrigued by.* The men in their crisp, sheetlike white dresses chatted with each other in Arabic, hailing cabs and smoking cigarettes, one after the other (cabs and cigarettes). The women floated in the background, shrouded in mystery, silently tending to children underfoot.

I was in Bahrain for a number of reasons, you could say, many of which would unfold over time, and none of which I was all that aware of on this first night. The most immediate and obvious reason I'd come to the Middle East was my Navy SEAL husband, Steve, whom I had married eight days earlier in San Diego.

Steve had already been living in Bahrain for a year, the first of a two-year tour. When he finished his first year, he flew home on leave and married me. After a short honeymoon near Lake Tahoe, we hopped on a jet bound for the other side of the world. We lived in Bahrain for the last year of Steve's tour, while he served as the operations officer of a SEAL Unit on the U.S. base.

I wanted to do the whole thing well. I wanted to be the right kind of wife for such a situation. I wanted to feel normal and at ease in this new place. None of those things were happening

---

*For Arabic word definitions, see pages 201–203.

found art

the way I had hoped, as I'm a five-foot-nine, fair-skinned, light-eyed blonde woman. I resembled nothing in my immediate surroundings, so slipping into the crowd as if I belonged simply wasn't an option.

In lieu of blending in, I dutifully followed my new husband to a cab, tripping over my bags as I juggled walking, toting luggage, and staring. I felt strangely visible and strangely invisible. I stuck out, but I wasn't getting much attention for it, except from a few young boys staring up at me from full-moon eyes. I wondered what they saw.

I arrived in Bahrain exhausted, numb even. My soul felt as though anesthesia had been poured directly into it. I lived a lifetime in just the anticipation of getting to Bahrain, and once there, I had no energy left to process. The fourteen months leading up to stepping off the plane had taken their toll, leaving me vacant.

When I made eye contact with the row of boys, I realized I was far, far away from home, and the familiar twinge of out-of-placeness crept up slowly at first and then gushed. The awkward adolescent Leeana instantly inhabited me — the one with big feet and big hands who bloomed impossibly early and always felt, with savage restlessness, like the ogre in a forest full of fairies.

Change is horribly uncomfortable. Like the wrong pair of jeans, change pinches and squeezes in the most inconvenient places. A lot of wriggling and writhing is involved. Maybe even some sucking in and prone posturing. Just when you think you've fit in, you realize you're spilling over the top and sides in the worst way. Very, very little ease.

If I would have had the energy on that first night, I might have thought more about where I would fit in, not only in a new country but in a new marriage, in my relationships back home, in the new relationships I would inevitably forge in Bahrain, in whatever awaited us after this tour was over, in my faith. I might have thought through the transition more carefully and intentionally and acknowledged that loss is the little sister who always tags along with change. All of this was far too much to process in the moment, however, and I succumbed to the disorientation.

A bigger picture—the one I was absolutely unable to see and the one we are all unable to see when we're overwhelmed by the immediate intensity of change—surely existed. In a very short time, I would begin to get glimpses of the divine metanarrative containing some important invitations for me, none of which I would have had the slightest bit of time for in the equilibrium and orientation and familiarity and comfort of my former life in San Diego.

Though I had lost some safety and belonging and planted-ness in this uprooting business, I had gained a great gift—imbalance. Not until I was set on my ear did I begin to see life a bit differently. The bigger picture exists each and every day, but normalcy (and a few other things we will get to) had dulled my senses. Imbalance, once I was able to survive the initial shock of it, began retuning my ears and refocusing my eyes, and life became literally breathtaking—as in, I was finally able to stop and *take* a real, live, sustaining *breath*.

Even on that first night, the new air, the new culture, the new language, the new husband, and the new land all whispered, in the lowest hush, of opportunity. If I could have willed myself to snap out of the mind-numbing exhaustion of change, if I could have willed myself to believe despite my unbelief that this awkward plucking had intention, I might have been more aware of and open to what was waiting for me. I had no such resources available. Maybe this means I'm disappointingly unspiritual, but I think it probably just means I'm human.

Standing on the curb of the Bahraini airport with luggage in hand, I had no idea that God himself was lurking in the Middle Eastern air, licking his chops (in a good way), just waiting for me to arrive with all my roots exposed and frayed.

Truthfully, I had no idea *anything* was waiting for me ...

Until I realized *Steve* was! Right next to a Gulf Cab he'd secured. I tried to navigate between the swarm of white *thobes* and black *abayas* that seemed to be dancing around me while I moved, slow motion, in and among them like a lost child winding her way through a band of street performers. They appeared regal and all dressed up. I, on the other hand, didn't, due to my beleaguered heart and jet-lagged tracksuit.

Steve was loading my year's worth of luggage into the trunk. What a good man. He had two wars on his hands — coordinating the SEAL operations in both Afghanistan and Iraq. He was incredibly overworked. The world was in chaos. And yet he loaded my bags, every last one of them, as if his only job was to be my husband.

"Capital Centre ..."

"On the other side of the Pearl Roundabout ..."

"Past the Gulf Hotel ..."

"Across the street from Mega Mart ..."

Steve delivered clues to the cab driver until he finally recognized our destination.

Though well after midnight, the cab driver still blasted Arabic techno with its distinct vocal warbling and clanging tambourines. A copy of the Qur'an slid around on the dash, while a circle of prayer beads kept time as it hit the windshield from its home on the rearview mirror. The cab driver talked on his cell phone and smoked during the entire drive to Capital Centre.

Soon the Gulf was in view. Then the tall silhouette of the white pearl set in four-story-high prongs that gave the Pearl Roundabout its name. Then the Gulf Hotel, packed with late-night partyers from all over the region. Then a few quick jogs, and we were sitting in front of our building—Capital Centre.

The Nepalese night watchman jumped out of his guard shack as our cab approached. He recognized Steve immediately and hurried back to the metal pole with the long rope tied to it, a less than impenetrable security system but one he takes very seriously. As he tugs at the rope on one end, the cinder block weighting the other end kicks in and the pole swings up so we can pass through into the ten- or twelve-spot parking lot our building shares with a few obscure retail shops.

"*Shukran*," Steve says, as the watchman helps us unload our bags from the trunk of the cab and reload them into the elevator. Steve slips him a *dinar* or two for his assistance.

"*Shukran*," the watchman says back, grinning. He appears happy to have Steve back. I'm sure he wonders who I am, though it seems by the grin he has it all figured out.

I, on the other hand, have nothing much figured out. The ropes, clips, fasteners, hooks, and, yes, roots that keep me so well tethered to my spot on the earth have come loose yet again, as they are apt to do in life. It is all I can do just to take in the Bahraini air.

loving

2

I met Steve the same week he returned from deployment
to the Middle East. He was supposed to deploy in January
2002, in which case we probably would never have met.
September 11, 2001, interrupted the world's plans and changed
everything—for us all. His platoon was called up early and left
just weeks after the terrorist attacks.

After seven months overseas, he walked off a C–5 onto
the tarmac of Naval Air Station North Island in San Diego,
just ten miles from where I lived. This was not his first time
in the city. He had been stationed in San Diego when he
went through BUD/S (Basic Underwater Demolition SEAL
Training), the infamously grueling preparation each SEAL
must endure—including the survival week known as Hell
Week. After completing the training, Steve received his Trident
(SEAL insignia pin) there on the San Diego beach as well.
After BUD/S, he was assigned to SEAL Team Three, which
headquartered in San Diego between deployments.

Five years in "the Teams" (as being in the SEAL teams is
often referred to)—ten miles away from each other the entire
time—and we never met. In fact, we even attended the same
church and shared a handful of mutual friends unknowingly.

Fate, with her droll humor, would have the last laugh. It wasn't until Steve took two-year orders to Bahrain, ten thousand miles away, that we finally met.

If I were to assign a phrase to my first impression of Steve, I would turn to the French, who, as usual, say it best: *coup de foudre*—literally translated, "a strike of thunder." This is what we might call "love at first sight" in English. At the time, I would have been embarrassed to admit such a thing, thinking those kinds of phrases were reserved for slightly desperate girls who go to a Christian college to look for a husband. Since it's all a done deal now, I'll fess up. I was struck—not a sappy, gooey struck, but an "I can't stop staring at that guy" kind of struck. Intrigued, in the way that you are intrigued by a car wreck or roadkill or someone collapsing in public. You want to turn away, but for some reason, you just can't.

Home from deployment only three days, Steve was sitting across the table from me at a conference we both happened to attend. I watched him, riveted. He kept reaching into a grocery store bag and pulling out individually wrapped pieces of gum. One after another. Unwrap, chew aggressively for no more than sixty seconds, spit out, reach back into the noisy plastic bag, and unwrap another.

His little sideshow was insanely distracting and strangely charming. He probably devoured thirty pieces of gum while I watched. I couldn't take my eyes off him. He had me at "chain chewing."

I wondered what kind of vice he was managing. No one wrecks an entire bag of bubble gum without some reason.

Chewing tobacco, I would later find out. He was trying to undo a nasty little habit he picked up on deployment. Possessing an addictive personality myself, I loved him from the start.

To this day, if our house gets really quiet, you can hear Steve shifting spit around in his mouth as if he were savoring some chew. His love affair with the stuff continues, though he quit some time ago. "The day they find a cure for cancer is the day I'm going out and getting myself some Copenhagen," he still swears.

We dated for seven whole weeks and then got engaged. When Steve asked me to marry him, I asked him three questions back: "Are you sure? Are you sure? Are you sure?" to which he replied in his Steve way: "Sometimes you just have to jump and trust your gear." He put a ring on my finger and left for Bahrain three weeks later.

How two people find each other is one of life's greatest mysteries, requiring a bit of luck, a bit of grace, and a bit of timing. Despite ourselves, Steve and I stumbled on to an enduring connection. In him, I saw someone honest whom I could trust. Steve's sins are not the sins of wooing or glad handing or insincerity. If anything, his are sins of omission, as he'd rather withhold truthfully than give disingenuously. I believe this quality, in addition to his come-hither, lagoon-green eyes, was the clincher. I felt safe.

Safety was ironic and important. Ironic because it would be the very thing literally threatened over and over again in our relationship. Important because I had spent an unfortunate amount of time in a previous relationship that was not so safe, and I was still a little banged up from that unlucky lack of judgment.

We were engaged on June 11, 2002. The world was in a strange spot just then. We were all still picking up the pieces from September 11, trying to figure out how to heal from our losses and our anger while the powers that be traded discussions on when to strike back. Rumors of war surfaced immediately, but it was some time before the plans would unfold. Though life seemed to return to relative normalcy on the surface, the undercurrent was unsettling. A storm seemed afoot, and as the world rumbled, my soul did too.

Soon after our engagement, I began feeling tense and unnerved. I was having trouble "trusting my gear." I surmised that trusting another person is one thing. Very frightening. But trusting *myself* with a decision of lifelong magnitude, that was another thing altogether. Believing in my own judgment was difficult, since I'd made a habit in the past of inviting in some pretty gnarly Wrong Ones. Letting in the Right One is difficult when you've made such mistakes. I was fumbling around with a loaded gun after proving myself to be a bit trigger-happy.

My inner turbulence drove me to all sorts of wild antics. I fretted and marched up a local mountain and yelled at God and kicked the dirt just to make a big scene. I made lunch appointments with my girlfriends to rehearse lists of the pros and cons for marrying Steve.

"He isn't Jesus Christ," my friend Linsey finally said to me rather pointedly, apparently tired of my nitpicking and fussing.

I called Steve in the middle of the night and cried into the phone for a mere two dollars a minute. I went and met with a woman in a room where we kneeled on pillows and prayed for freedom and space and a sense that the walls weren't closing in. I begged God for one freaking second of peace.

Peace came in the form of truth, as it often does. After rehearsing every conceivable fear and foible I could possibly drum up, I finally realized that Steve was never going to be perfect. I also realized that his love for me was never going to be perfect either. Shortly thereafter, it *also* dawned on me that my

found art

love for him would be radically imperfect as well. That is when I realized the quandary of love.

I've felt abandoned. I've felt rejected. I've felt abused. All of these are difficult to endure. Perhaps the *most* difficult, ironically, is feeling loved. Giving up on, walking away from, or sabotaging a good thing—these are all easier options than loving. Truly letting someone in entirely and enduring their desire to love you, knowing they will love so imperfectly, is really very difficult. We will let each other down terribly. We will hurt each other in the process of trying to love each other. We will have to endure flawed love. This is quite a dilemma.

I found an ounce more peace when I realized that Jesus' twelve best friends were a bunch of narcoleptic, betraying doubters whom he loved and stuck with despite their shortcomings. He saw the good in them beyond the bad, and he let them sit very close to him, even though they asked dumb questions and were annoying at times. That is grace, the most primary and necessary ingredient in love.

Loving has nothing to do with getting it right all the time. Loving—the real deal that only God can help us do—always protects, always trusts, always hopes, always perseveres. That kind of gracious loving never fails. Your parachute might. But love ... never love.

holding on

3

People ask me all the time what it's like being married to a Navy SEAL. Most marriages, I suspect, have aspects that seem foreign and strange to others but seem normal and usual to those in the situation. In other words, much of what Steve and I have experienced together has become our normal, though it may appear to be anything but that to those looking in.

If I had to put into words what makes our marriage distinct, I could mention any number of highlights. Our very abbreviated courtship, for one thing. Though it might not seem related at first glance, I do attribute our seven-week dating relationship to Steve's job. In the SEAL world, everything is a mission. I might also mention that our entire fourteen-month engagement was spent long-distance, and I wouldn't want to leave out the fact that two wars started during our engagement, which meant there were plenty of times in those early days of our relationship when I had absolutely no idea where in the world he was or what in the world he was doing.

Aside from all those things and the semiautomatic firearms, cases of ammunition, and multiple sets of body armor sitting in our closets; aside from the unplanned trips to the far reaches of the universe (can you say Djibouti?); aside from living with a professional pirate who can weave baskets, make traps from tree bark, and survive in the wild for months; and aside from all the classified stories I can't ever know—aside from all that, it's pretty much a run-of-the-mill marriage.

On a deeper level, being married to a SEAL has filleted my heart wide open and has made me, over time, uncomfortably vulnerable. You'd think that being married to someone so stereotypically strong, brave, and capable would make me feel completely protected and safe. In some senses, this is true. I'm a better flyer when I fly with Steve. I'm not afraid of anyone breaking into our house or coming after us in a dark alley. As I've already testified to, I certainly feel emotionally safe with him. But there's a different sphere of vulnerability in our relationship that I became acquainted with before we ever took our vows.

At any moment, a phone call, a knock on my door, or a story on the news could change my life forever. That knowledge shades every passing moment with vulnerability, a reminder that life is not in my control.

I received my initial education on this searing vulnerability about halfway through our engagement. In late 2002, Steve had been in Bahrain working with an advanced planning team that was looking at the different logistical scenarios for invading Iraq. Of course, I didn't know any of this. At the time, all such information was classified.

President George Bush had just given Hussein his WMD* ultimatum, and the clock was ticking. Hussein, who had been playing a high-stakes game of cat and mouse, needed to allow United Nations inspectors unfettered access to Iraqi plants and

---

*Weapons of mass destruction.

manufacturing facilities or Bush was going to invade. Steve knew Bush wasn't bluffing. Hundreds of military hours had already been dedicated to planning the invasion. All that was left was the word from Bush.

Steve came home from Bahrain about that time so we could celebrate Thanksgiving together. I will never forget the look in his eyes when he said to me, "I wish there was some other way to fix this thing than going to war. No one wants war."

The possibility of war was not entirely unexpected. The temperature had been rising on every news channel for months as pundits anticipated and speculated, each with their own spin. We all began to face the complicated reality of entering into such a historical fight amid divided and contesting opinions. While the rest of us were getting bits and pieces on the news, Steve had been sitting in this reality for months, and his look told me more than his words did.

I was living in a completely different world, naively preoccupied with becoming a bride. It never occurred to me that Saddam Hussein would mess with that.

We set our wedding date for August, and Steve flew back to Bahrain. Shortly after, Hussein continued to balk, so Bush gave the high sign and moved U.S. military personnel into position.

With no warning, Steve went totally missing. After Thanksgiving, I put him on a commercial flight back to Bahrain, and I didn't hear a single word from him until February 14, Valentine's Day. I think he knew he'd be off the grid for some time, which is why he was serious and weighed down when I saw him. I, on the other hand, had no warning, no clue. The whole mess hit me very suddenly, and I was painfully aware of how little information I had been given.

I walked around with glazed eyes most of that time — a

survival mechanism I would get good at over time. I became acquainted quickly with the mind-numbing soul paralysis that soon became a regular, uninvited guest.

On Valentine's Day 2003, I received a postcard from Steve that pictured the island of Cyprus with a simple message on the back about missing me and loving me, no mention of why he was in Cyprus or what he was doing there. Later that day, he called me on a satellite phone, and we struggled to understand each other through the delayed signal. The conversation was convoluted, and I asked way too many specific questions, surely threatening national security more than a few times in those eight brief minutes.

I picked up on the fact that I wasn't going to get a printout of Steve's travel itinerary as long as he was on his way to invade another country. That kind of specificity just wasn't practical. We had a few more stilted conversations in which I learned he was aboard the HMS *Ocean*, a British aircraft carrier where he was serving as a liaison officer to Royal Marines.

Because he couldn't talk about much more than what he ate every day, I decided to fill the space with some wedding business. In retrospect, I probably could have been a bit more sensitive to the milieu of our relationship, but brides are a compulsively focused species.

"Hey honey, I booked the florist today," I said. "What do you think about all pink flowers?"

"I don't know, sweetie," Steve said. "I'm in the middle of trying to keep World War Three from happening. Thanks for wanting to include me in every excruciating detail. You know how important this wedding is to me. It's right there on my calendar after Going to War."

I got a taste of my own medicine as people began asking me a litany of inane questions.

"So have you heard from him?"
"Where is he?"
"Do you think they have him doing something top secret?"
"Does he believe Iraq has WMDs?"
"What does he think of George W.?"

I patiently tolerated most inquiries, but then they'd ask the worst, the most hostile, of them all:

"Do you think he'll even be able to come home for the wedding?"

"I don't know," I'd reply (at least to myself). "I'll have to give him a call and see what he thinks. Oh, wait. I have no number to reach him. I have no address to send mail to. The last time I heard from him was a cryptic communication from the island of Cyprus. But yes, I do believe he'll be home for this wedding, or I'm calling Saddam personally."

Though we all prayed that Hussein would somehow cooperate with Bush's requests and spare us all the disaster of war, there was no such luck.

I stood in the San Diego airport waiting to board a flight to visit Steve's parents in the Bay Area when Operation Iraqi Freedom began. No one knew exactly when the first artillery would fire, but the entire country was stressed and pinched, waiting for the word. In the terminal, crowds of people were gathered around—all silent—as the news reporter announced that we were officially at war.

Some people immediately cheered as the television showed Patriots intercepting Iraqi missiles and rockets and offensive fire in the forms of Tomahawks and JDAMs careening into

Baghdad. *Shock and awe* was about to become a national catchphrase overnight.

I had nothing to cheer about. My conflictedness was undoubtedly observable. I had no way of hiding how pensive and vulnerable I felt. I wonder if that's a bit of how we all felt in those days. War is a triumph for no one. Hundreds of people surrounded me, each with their own take on things, none of whom had any clue how closely connected I was to the war. In the crowd at San Diego International Airport, I felt deeply alone.

When I arrived in Northern California, Steve's mom, Joanie, produced two tickets to *Les Misérables.* I'm not sure either of us was prepared for the poignancy of watching that musical on that particular day.

The French Revolution is in full steam, and the streets of France are war-torn and ravaged. Jean Valjean, the main character, has left his daughter at home to go out and look for her love, Marius, who has gone into the fight and not returned.

As Valjean searches the back alleys of France for Marius, my heart pounded. After he discovers Marius's injured body, we watched as Valjean trudges through the underground sewer passages with Marius in his arms, the sounds of war raging through the opera house.

Jean Valjean thinks of his daughter, Cosette, at home, waiting to hear that her Marius is alive. He sings out the gut-wrenching chorus "Bring Him Home," and I sank into my seat with tears running down my face. I was embarrassed that Joanie might see me crying, and I was embarrassed that I was so scared and stunned by all the day's events. I was embarrassed at how naive I had been, thinking I was living some romantic fairy tale.

If there had been such a fairy tale, the frivolous romance had most certainly and most abruptly ended.

Outside the playhouse, we fought through a crowd of protestors carrying huge antiwar signs. I was dizzy with disbelief. Even more so when we got in the car. On the way home from the theatre we heard a news report on the radio that a helicopter carrying Coalition forces and one U.S. Navy officer had gone down in the Gulf—no survivors. It seemed as though every helicopter we had was falling out of the sky during that first week of the war. The last I had heard, Steve was one of the few U.S. officers aboard that ship. The disorienting disbelief was compounded with blinding fear.

We drove back to Steve's parents' house and watched the news while I cried. We just sat helplessly waiting for the phone or the doorbell to ring. They never did. No word from the Navy, and no word from Steve. My last correspondence with him might as well have been a lifetime ago.

That night, I fell asleep in my future in-laws' guest room right next to a picture of Steve taken on the day he was born. In the middle of the night, I woke up—still groggy from all my tears—and I stumbled into the hallway. I ran my hand along the wall until I found the framed picture of Steve from the Naval Academy, uniformed and young. Looking into his green eyes, I told him he better come home for me.

Exhausted and terrified, I returned to San Diego and waited. Within days, an email from Steve confirmed his safety. He had left the ship prior to the crash and had been forward, participating in the invasion.

Months later, after we were married and living in Bahrain for some time, I recounted that weekend to Steve. He disappeared for a bit and then returned with a small piece of lined, green notebook paper. *19 March 2003* was written at the top — the very same weekend I sat in the playhouse in San Francisco wondering where he could be.

The note read:

> Gas attack. False alarm. Big sandstorm. Storm might preclude any ops tonight. Wish I could be with you. Things just seem so far away. I have a hard time remembering what it was like to be away from this. I just hope we all have a time when this whole thing is a faded memory.
>
> Wind seems to be picking up — shifted from southeast to northwest. The guys are really keen to get on with the job and then get home.
>
> I love you. Me.

He was sitting in Kuwait when he wrote those few words to me, suited up in body armor and climbing in and out of biohazard gear in the middle of sandstorm winds as the ground shook from Patriot missiles.

A few months later, in August, he was able to break away from the world's stage just long enough to come home on leave, look into my eyes, and make a vow:

> *I, Steve, take you, Leeana, to be my wife,*
> *To have and to hold,*
> *From this day forward,*
> *For better, for worse,*
> *For richer, for poorer,*
> *In sickness and in health,*
> *To love and to cherish,*
> *Until we are parted by death.*
> *As God is my witness, I give you my promise.*

Eight days later, we boarded a plane—this time together—and disappeared to another world.

Ours has never been a connection of convenience or ease. Love is rarely, if ever, convenient. I might even go so far as to say that convenient love isn't really love at all. When we said those vows, we had no way of knowing what would unfold over the coming months and years. Unplanned deployments, burying SEAL teammates, the fear of losing my once-in-a-lifetime person—none of these were on the radar. We had no idea how it would feel to hold on to a marriage in the midst of such vulnerable and threatening circumstances.

One of the very hardest things I have done in my life is face the fears associated with loving Steve. I have come to the conclusion that a few things are worth holding on to no matter what is required—a dream, a relationship, faith. The hard part is, sometimes you can't see or touch or feel the dream, or the person, or God, and you have to believe anyway. I have spent many a night in a bed by myself, married to thin air, more or less. Something inside me, though, continues. Maybe I have learned the power of commitment. Maybe I have learned the power of stubbornness. Maybe because of, not in spite of, all this craziness, I have learned the power of believing.

a braid of fringe
from a persian rug

4
war

Steve extended his leave long enough to get me settled before he had to return to work — cell phone, base identification card, a driving tour of the city's main attractions, and a walking tour of the base. He provided me with a pocket-sized, neon-green notebook full of directions to any of the major errands I might need to run. He taught me how to navigate the full-service gas stations, asking for *mumtaz* when I pulled in. He pointed out the grocery store across the street — Mega Mart, if you can possibly imagine such an obscenely Westernized name — and he filled my wallet with Bahraini *dinar* and *fils* and reminded me of the exchange rate.

As soon as these cursory introductions were made, Steve disappeared back to his work — as if the rapture had occurred — and I was left alone. It was the kind of alone I hadn't experienced in recent memory. Not only was there no one physically present with me throughout my day, but there was no one to call, no one to visit, no one to meet for lunch. No one except me. Me, and the beer and beef jerky in the fridge. Since I couldn't come up with anything edible to make for dinner out of those two ingredients, I decided to venture out to the store. The party wasn't going to come to me.

Capital Centre was the flat Steve selected when he first moved to Bahrain. Low on some of the things a woman might notice or prefer, the building was old but not classic, more peculiar than interesting, and ever-smelling of curry and other people's furniture.

I chose to believe Steve selected Capital Centre not because of the insides so much as the location—directly across the King Faisal Highway from the most spellbinding stretch of the Persian Gulf. From our master bedroom window, you could see all the way out to the horizon, and our disproportionately huge, sand-swept patio extended far enough to cover the view of the highway so that our flat felt perched on top of the Gulf. When I started to feel as though the strange smells of Capital Centre were seeping into my skin, I pulled back the heavy forest-green drapes covering our master bedroom window and watched for the beating heart that sat right under the surface of the Gulf. The flat's offenses were immediately assuaged.

A meat market was next door to Capital Centre, a strategic location for the fishermen to wheelbarrow in the fresh catch from their *dhows* before dawn. The August heat mixed with the dead fish, and I was slapped in the face with the smell of raw cat food as I exited Capital Centre and headed out for groceries.

Immediately, I was interested in the sea of shadowy black *abayas* pouring into the meat market. So much so that I stopped and watched instead of crossing the street and heading directly to Mega Mart. Workmen carrying huge hunks of raw flesh pushed past the *abayas* and disappeared into the building. One carried a skinned lamb over his shoulders with the feet chopped off, making me think of the picture of Jesus carrying the lost sheep back to the fold.

The women shopping at the meat market were different from

the women I noticed in other parts of town, say, the Seef Mall. The Seef Mall women were decorated with henna and dripping with gold, and their bejeweled *abayas* concealed Western clothes and expensive shoes. In their presence, I felt perpetually underdressed. My Southern California-inspired flip-flops and denim seemed childish next to their floor-length black silk gowns. I watched them sit on the stools at the M.A.C. counter and have elaborate eye makeup applied in peacock-feather greens and purples. They drove themselves around in expensive cars without male escorts, showpieces of prosperity and progressive Islam.

The women at the meat market are not these women. Their lives do not ring of wealth or outside influence. They signal religious tradition and ancient custom. The hemlines of their *abayas* are dusty and unadorned, and their entire faces are covered with black veils. These women are not allowed to drive or go anywhere without a male relative. They do not laugh with each other over lattes. They are dark and silent and appear to have neither time for nor interest in anything other than the food they've come to purchase.

The women of Bahrain intrigued me with their disparate lives all cloaked in blackness. They didn't seem real to me much of the time. Either they were token beauties, lovely but ignored, or they were shadowy specters, shrouded and faceless.

I stood out in the August heat and became increasingly interested in the meat market, not exactly sure if I was welcome or not. Would someone ask me to leave? Would anyone speak English? Would I know how to barter for my purchases? Would I even know what to buy? What would I do with an entire skinned lamb?

Mega Mart, and again I emphasize the lunacy of the name,

was the grocery store I was supposed to patronize, the place where I *should* shop. Stocking my fridge there made so much more sense. The meat had been butchered and wrapped in Styrofoam and Saran Wrap instead of carried to the car on someone's shoulders in one big piece. I found it hard to argue with a store that offered clear price tags, checkout clerks who spoke English, and coolers of cold Coke Light.

Standing in the middle of the street, trying to decide if I would succumb to the safety of Mega Mart or run headlong into the adventure of the meat market, I wished I were so much braver than I actually am. I wished I were the type of person who sees the entire world as her place and makes no apologies for shouldering into every corner she wants to experience. Along with this honest musing is the wish to be so much less concerned with what other people are thinking of me. These perceived judgments keep me paralyzed.

I am hardly a brave person. I am the kind of person who, at any moment, is anxiously overcompensating for strange insecurities such as . . .

- wishing I knew more about music.
- wishing I knew how to cook well.
- wishing I had really learned a foreign language—not just faked my way through Spanish.
- wishing I were up-to-date on blogging.
- wishing I were like so-and-so (any one of my friends whom I perceive to be better equipped for such an adventure).
- wishing I had slightly thinner ankles.

Then, and only then, would I feel at ease, or even (God forbid) brave. When these insecurities stir, I begin to believe the toxic voices that tell me I'm the only one feeling off and odd and that everyone else is at perfect peace in their particular skin.

I am a fitful, self-conscious person who wants to be wild but who bows in the face of fear. Iraq is just two hundred miles away from this patch of concrete I am standing on, but that isn't the war most prevalent on my mind at the moment. The war I'm fighting is the epic battle of myself against myself—a bruising, losing sort of war (as all war is) that I can't seem to shake loose from.

Steve says the days of army-versus-army warfare are over. We saw the last of such conventionality in World War II. Now we face an elusive enemy of guerillas and insurgents on a muddled battlefield with no clear lines or rules or boundaries. I can relate. I am so often stepping into land mines of my own insecurities and shame, never quite sure where the enemy will pop up. Being out of place is always a trigger.

I remember being twenty-two and arriving in Morgantown, West Virginia, for my first semester of graduate school. All of a sudden, I was the only person in the entire world who didn't smoke. Literally the entire world. Tragically, I assumed I would never be able to fit in because, due to my lifelong struggle with asthma, I was going to have to give up on smoking before I ever started.

Turns out, smoking, per se, wasn't so much what I was longing for. I've since learned that we're rarely longing for the obvious thing we think we're longing for. Usually, the longing is a much deeper thing we have to discover after some wandering and angst. So every smoke break, I wandered around Stansbury Hall, the old brick building where all my classes met, and tried to find what everyone else was doing while the smokers smoked.

But — and this is where the angst would set in — there was no one left.

After some time, it occurred to me that what I was really longing for was to be a part of the smoking *culture*, a culture made up of bohemian graduate students who puffed clouds of sweet-smelling cloves on the landing of Stansbury Hall and smartly discussed literary criticism in a language I could not understand. These were the students who really belonged in graduate school. They easily and coolly exchanged jocular stories with professors in a way that spoke of camaraderie and confidence. They wore handmade jewelry and vintage clothing and gardened and somehow found the time and desire to read copiously, far beyond their assigned texts. I felt like a wannabe in their presence. I hid inside, nursing a Coke (before I realized girls drink Diet), wishing I could play even just a small role in the clove romance.

What I was really, really longing for was the sense that I fit, that I belonged.

Finally, one evening during a break in our class, I bravely wandered out to the landing and sat down on the edge of the collective chimney. I listened as I inhaled large quantities of secondhand smoke and tried for all I was worth to pick up on the mother tongue. Though the risk was painful, and I felt insecure and small and childish with my can of Coke and my out-of-place naïveté, I kept going out to the landing to see what all the hubbub was about. Each entry onto the Stansbury stoop gave me confidence, and pretty soon, those iconic students noticed me and made space for me and even attempted to include me in their eternally brainy conversations.

This must have been when I fell in love with the smell of

found art

cloves. To this day, the distinct aroma reminds me of the crisp mountain air of Morgantown during fall and of belonging.

My neuroses have resurfaced in Bahrain, I'm afraid. I believe I've heard a saying about that—something to the effect of, "Everywhere you go, there you are." I find myself battling the same old demons, who are by now far too familiar company.

In the end, I decided to walk to Mega Mart, a cop-out by some standards. The heat was rising, and I needed a Coke Light in the worst way.

The rattle of my ungreased shopping cart wheels cued a row of black mounds sitting on the ground near the exit of Mega Mart. Instantly, wrinkled palms outstretched in my direction, jutting out from black fabric. No eyes, no mouths, no faces. Just empty palms connected to black ghosts—all huddled and hunched there at my feet.

"Shi'a widows," Steve later explains. "They're always out there begging."

Our neighborhood abuts a Shi'a village, where the Bahraini have-nots live. The Shi'a are the disenfranchised of the two Islamic denominations. The Sunni are the minority ruling party. They possess the money and the palaces, though they represent only a handful of powerful families. The Shi'a are the majority, but many live in slumlike conditions in poor villages and are far removed from the trade money that has brought Bahrain most of its wealth.

I dug into my purse, searching for a few *fils*, and I dropped a coin into each hand. The fingers immediately closed, grasping the coin, and then disappeared back into the fabric again.

On my walk back to Capital Centre, I passed the meat

market and felt shamed by my cold drink and packaged meats. I tried to blame my cowardice on the fact that I was raised Baptist and therefore was repressed. Most Baptists probably wouldn't go into the meat market. Too messy and risky. Most Baptists would tend toward something, anything, in Saran Wrap. Much, much safer. Blame shifting made me feel at least a little bit better, for the moment.

I also tried to compensate for the feeling of failure by believing that someday I would gather the courage to enter the meat market. "Hope," Steve often reminds me, "isn't a strategy," but such wishful thinking seemed easier than other, more invasive analyses.

I also tried — or, more accurately, thought to try — to give myself some grace in this new land, but that moment of spiritual sanity was lambasted by my loathsome self-talk. I tried to pray out the lies and pray in the truth. I tried to think of Psalm 139 and remember how fearfully and wonderfully I am made. I tried to fight with the very few weapons I could think to wield. All these efforts were difficult, though, and my own personal war continued to rage. I was as poor in spirit as the Shi'a widows outside Mega Mart. I was reaching up and out from behind the shrouded mystery of my own soul, asking for a gift.

found art

5
quit searching

Stupid, stupid fly. The beastly insect just kept banging his head
against the Plexiglas wall in the middle of the common area
right outside our flat. I opened the front door to head to the
elevator, and all I could hear was his angry buzz.

A strange storage area sat directly beyond the front door
of our flat. Four Plexiglas walls—floor to ceiling—created a
makeshift landfill that I passed whenever I left. Capital Centre
didn't exactly have a system for garbage collection, so the storage
area provided a convenient depository for all sorts of odds and
ends. A collection of random refuse, including old appliances,
trash bags, and discarded furniture, had accumulated and
attracted this crazy fly.

The fly was really big, maybe the largest I'd ever seen, and he
was acting as though he was trapped inside the storage area. He
reared back, put his head down, and flew face-first into the wall
in front of him. He did it again and again, gaining no ground,
though he was doing his best to find some crack or seam he
might manage to break through. He was resilient, but the brutal
force with which he was hurling himself into the wall was taking
its toll.

On the other side of the storage area, behind where the fly

was attempting his escape, I noticed a full-sized door standing wide open. Any human, much less any fly, could have passed through the opening with ease. Too bad the fly had no idea what was directly behind him. If he just turned around and looked, he would realize that freedom was so close.

I watched the fly for at least a couple of minutes, which is a long time if you're just watching a fly. He seemed scared and angry, searching for something he was never going to find by facing the direction he was facing.

Before I headed to the elevator, I noticed he was slowing down a bit. Maybe he was about to die. I wasn't sure. As the elevator doors closed, I could still hear his angry buzz, stopping and starting, as he ran headlong into the Plexiglas wall. Even a fly will die trying to get away from all the garbage.

Garbage—the need to be thought well of, the need to prove myself to a world that requires no convincing, the fear of imperfection, the insatiable desire to be worthy—was piled up in my life, as evidenced in my earliest forays into my new surroundings.

Though I couldn't have told you exactly where the bags came from or why I was living in their stench, I knew the garbage was there and that it had been there for some time. The problem was, I hadn't yet decided if I was ready to be free from the familiar companionship of shame, fear, and perfectionism.

I came to Bahrain much more like that fly than I wanted to admit. I knew I wanted out of the garbage-filled room in theory, but I had been planning my escape on my own terms, which had (for years) involved the head-splitting flailings of managing and striving. Despite my best attempts to do better and be more, I was so very stuck.

Feeling stuck is scary.

I was particularly stuck at the end of my college days. I began dating a guy, and I got all turned around—so turned around, in fact, that I didn't even recognize myself when I looked in the mirror. I was a phantom self who had fallen prey to charm and adventure instead of paying attention to the red flags that waved from early on.

I genuinely assumed only meth addicts and prostitutes got themselves into destructive relationships. Surely well-intentioned Christian college graduates with good grooming and relatively nice families wouldn't—no, *couldn't*—land themselves squarely in such a mess. This assumption, no matter how sincere, proved costly.

My gross underestimation of the situation caused a dangerous devolution that cost me my bearings. A particular man became a controlling man. A controlling man became a volatile man. A volatile man became an unsafe man.

As the degeneration unfolded bit by bit, I felt up to the task of fixing someone else's huge, gaping wounds by ignoring my own. The truth is, fixing just isn't that great of a day job—mainly because you end up getting broken in the process. Both of us had raw and tangled pain—mine deeply buried, and his red-hot on the surface—and we each needed something the other couldn't provide, though we continuously asked it of each other with brutal audacity.

I banged my head against a Plexiglas wall, sure that somehow, if I just rammed myself into it hard enough, a crack would appear, and things would change. All the while, a huge door stood wide open right behind me—an exit—but I just wouldn't turn around and look at it.

Why?

I've asked myself that question more than a few hundred

times. Why was I so willing to sacrifice myself for the sake of wishful thinking? The only answer I can come up with has to do with my empty hope for redemption.

Once I lost my emotional well-being and sacrificed my personal convictions, a certain momentum began to build, and all of a sudden it seemed too late to get out. I'd already invested so much—how could I walk away? What if we just needed one more week or one more month or one more year to really get things on track? Wouldn't I be glad I'd hung in there? Wouldn't it all be worth it then?

The great lie was that throwing good emotional energy after bad, good time after bad, good hope after bad, would somehow allow me to salvage what was lost. Instead, I discovered a harsh truth: what was gone was gone, and trying to redeem my losses by losing more just didn't add up. I was simply banging my head against a very solid wall.

After two long years, a sliver of clarity presented itself. I finally allowed a dash of truth in. That's all it takes. I gave myself permission to admit that this was not a man I was willing to raise children with, and soon after that revelation, I ended it. Despite all the reasons that breaking off our relationship should have been a no-brainer, choosing to walk away remains one of the most difficult decisions I've ever made. I was high on the drug of false intimacy. I was used to being strung out, and I was reduced and wasted from using. I had been on a search that yielded nothing but pain, and though the door to freedom stood wide open behind me, I was dead set on making the whole thing work my way. I wanted sobriety—but never bad enough to turn around and fly.

I'd spent large amounts of time on a search for something— love, worth, affirmation, acceptance—only to discover that I'd been searching in all the wrong places. My own efforts left me circling, looking for life on my own terms, when what I really needed to do was quit searching for a loophole or an exception or my own way.

The day I watched that fly catapult himself into the Plexiglas wall, I too was bruised and trapped from trying to escape my own issues. Somewhere deep inside me, however, I knew that the door was wide open behind me. I knew God was offering me another way. An invitation hung in the rotten air, and I desperately wanted freedom.

keeping silence

I know people who like to go to the desert for entertainment.
They take their sand toys to Borrego Springs or Ocotillo Wells
or Glamis or any of the other deserts right outside San Diego,
and they run dune buggies and sleep in their motor homes.
This kind of weekending is of no interest to me. I am not much
into cactus and coyotes and dream-catcher earrings. The only
redeeming thing I can think of when it comes to deserts is that
they always seem to be close to casinos, and I do love casinos.

Because the desert is foreign to me, living in one was weird,
something that took getting used to. Living in an ancient desert
was weirder yet. Right outside my flat was the Bible-times desert
where people endured intense experiences such as temptations
from the devil, murder, slavery, fasting, eating locusts, cursing
God, and/or dying. That desert was a far cry from full moons
and slot machines.

One of the austere desert qualities I noticed right away
was the relentless wind. In the late summer and early fall, the
Shamal rips down from Iraq and kicks up so much sand that
the sun is all but eclipsed. One man is said to have reported
that the Shamal peeled the paint right off his car, but I can't
confirm the story.

I met the Shamal one night when it rattled my windows with the hellish fury of a deranged cat trying to claw its way up a chalkboard, scratching and screeching. I thought my building—and, by proxy, me—was a goner for sure. Being from earthquake country, I should have thought to go stand in a doorway or something, but panic made me dive off the couch and onto the floor in the middle of the living room. I lay there for some time with my heart in my mouth, waiting for the storm to pass. The wind howled late into the night, and the next morning, the landscape looked like a giant wooden spoon had come down from heaven and stirred everything up.

Trash was everywhere, littering the shoreline of the Gulf, blowing across the streets, dancing in the waves. Boulder-sized pocks were opened in the road, huge dunes were constructed overnight, patio furniture was long gone. A fine layer of silty sand covered absolutely everything in my flat, including the dining room table, the clothes and shoes in my closet, and the bowl of apples in the kitchen. I even felt it on my skin when I woke up the next morning, and I crunched little invisible granules in my teeth like you do when you go to the beach.

Despite the severity of the Middle Eastern desert, people seem to come to it looking for something—a promised land, a treasure, an escape, a reformation of the soul. None of this is lost on me. The Israelites of the Old Testament Scriptures came to the desert to wander. Of course, that wasn't their plan. They thought it would merely be an escape route from slavery to their homeland, the Promised Land. Wrong. The desert became their adopted home, a place of incoherent wandering for forty years. The only good thing they got out of the desert was a bit of manna and some hard-won lessons.

The Desert Mothers and Fathers of the third, fourth, and

fifth centuries came to the desert to live in total asceticism, away from the effects of the Roman Empire on the Christian church. They wanted separateness, radical worship, and a lifestyle of zealous discipleship. Theirs was a search for simplicity and reform in the wastelands of Egypt and Syria—a lifestyle as extreme as the landscape they chose.

I'm sure I'm here to wander a bit, though I hate to admit it. Wandering is so dang tiresome and circular. (The Israelites are giving me a resounding "Amen!" right now.) I hate having to revisit and relearn and return. Wandering seems so futile. I prefer MapQuest directions and clearly marked signage. If I've learned anything at all, I've learned that life surely doesn't work that way.

Like the Desert Mothers and Fathers, I'm sure I'm also here to live apart from the mainstream for a season. I've never really thought of myself as the monk type. In fact, there have been times in my life when sitting alone with myself has felt like the social equivalent of making incessant small talk with a perfect stranger. In response, I've made a habit out of filling up most every quiet moment with at least a little bit of noise—enough to keep me distracted from the discomfort of not really knowing myself.

The deserts of Bahrain offer me an alternative. Solitude.

At first, I had no idea what to do with such a gift. I went about the task of writing two billion thank-you notes for gifts we received from our wedding. I began washing camouflaged uniforms in the strange European washer/dryer combo in our kitchen at Capital Centre. I went on base to check my email because we couldn't get Internet access in our flat. I painted my toenails, plucked my eyebrows, ironed the newly washed uniforms, purchased a broom and tinfoil and lemon pepper at

Mega Mart, squeezed in a nap or two, finished reading Phyllis Tickle's memoir by the pool on base, and sent a few dozen text messages to Steve while he was trying to work. All of this took about three days, and then I was back at Capital Centre, all alone with myself once again.

The silence was deafening, and I was painfully aware of it ringing all around me. The quiet was so foreign that I didn't even know where to start—evidence that *I* was also very foreign to me.

Often life becomes a big, whirling cloud of chaos, picking up momentum—not to mention patio furniture and car paint—as it goes. The crazy dervish bangs on our windows and scratches and claws at our door and leaves a gritty residue on us when we're looking the other way. Life, the very thing we're supposed to be living, is pounding on the panes of our souls, and there we are, lying on the living room floor waiting for the windows to give way.

The winds of life had dug out huge pocks in my heart and deposited "get it done now" and "you've got to prove yourself" and "don't show a flaw" where living flesh had once been. Who was I underneath all that debris?

Like a bad first date, I awkwardly started about the task of figuring out who might be hiding inside my skin. I began by simply enjoying something I wanted to enjoy in a way that looked more like *being* instead of *doing*. I pulled back the forest-green polyester drapes of the master bedroom, and I stood there and stared out toward the Gulf, noticing everything between me and the horizon—the pairs of white *thobes* and black *abayas* strolling down the boardwalk, the *corniche* at the water's edge, the *dhows* dipping way out against the skyline, the tips of the water frothing up like meringue in the wind, the row of palms outlining the *corniche* shuttering gracefully.

The collective rhythm was like hypnotherapy, and I watched and watched until I could hear myself breathing again.

The only noise I allowed in was my first friend in Bahrain — Richard the BBC reporter. I'd occasionally pipe him in for some company. He would recount the woes of the world through British teeth, coating it all with enough wit and sarcasm to make the horse pill of war somewhat more tolerable.

My world was huge and endless, like the never-ending horizon on the other end of the Gulf. There were limitless options. This reality was equally freeing and frightening. My world was also very small and quiet, almost completely contained within the concrete walls of Capital Centre. This, too, was equally freeing and frightening.

Who was I apart from my job, my family, my friends, and even my church? Who was I without the trappings of achieving and striving? What was at the core of me? No assumptions. No pretenses. No one watching. No one expecting. No editing. No proving. Who was the Leeana behind and beneath and beyond the opinions of others, the cool competence, and the busyness?

The risk of sitting in the silence, as we all know, is what we will find there. I began to see the props I had been leaning on for quite some time. With these crutches exposed, I saw the hitches and limps for what they really were.

I had to start really small so as not to overwhelm myself. Every day, I put my list away, pulled the drapes back, and watched the water. One day, I forgot to turn on BBC and didn't even realize it. Little by very little, I practiced the discipline of silence. I didn't know that's what I was doing at the time. I stumbled onto it, actually. I wandered around and around that flat like sandstorm winds until it became obvious there was nothing left to do except quiet down.

I got quiet. And then I got quieter. And then I got silent. That's when the magic happened. I began to keep good company with myself, the kind of company you would keep with a friend instead of an enemy.

With time, Capital Centre became a place for me, a holy place you could say. Not just a place to cook meals or do laundry or complete tasks, but a place to *be*. The spacious quiet started working on the inaccessible, lost parts of me like a good massage. The silence reached down into the depths where the truest me resided, as if someone put their hands on me and made me feel the presence of my own skin where I had so recently been just bare bones. I was given a sense of myself that I had not experienced previously.

My friend Wanida can sing like the sun. Really. Her voice is radiant, filling up a room with power and heat and intensity. But when she was in college, her voice turned on her. She found out that she had nodes on her vocal chords that needed immediate attention if she were to salvage her singing voice. The doctors recommended months of voice rest, so Wanida complied, tapping on phone receivers, writing on notepads, and signing and signaling as best she could. Months of total silence. After some time, the doctors decided she was a good candidate for surgery, but the recovery from the surgery was more months of voice rest. She went about it again — tapping, gesturing, writing, mouthing. More silence. At the end of the voice rest and the surgery and the voice rest again, Wanida's voice came back. This time, the sound was different. What emerged from her lungs, her vocal chords, and her mouth was a much stronger, resonant, enduring voice. Bigger and better than it had ever been.

Sometimes we need silence. Not always, but definitely sometimes. If we will comply, if we will receive the moments of quiet contemplation and rest, we might be surprised by what emerges. As much as I didn't want to engage in the art of shutting up, the solitude offered me gifts I had never, ever received.

Like a desert windstorm, life is often unruly—wild, fierce, and howling. By choosing the stiller and smaller world of voice rest and life rest and mind rest and body rest, I somehow chose the stiller, smaller voice of God.

Though the desert was strange and unfamiliar to me most of the time, I believe God provided a present-day manna amid its desolation. Soul nourishment. Even the Shamal can't take that away.

7
healing

When you live somewhere totally foreign, you have to make
a decision. Are you going to be a tourist or a resident? This
dilemma presents itself often. If you are a tourist, then
you can experience your surroundings lightly and almost
dismissively, because, after all, your primary goal is most likely
entertainment. On the other hand, if you are a resident, then
you have work to do. You have to go about the task of making a
place that is unknown known. Becoming familiar to a place and
allowing that place to become familiar to you take time and a
commitment to exploration.

The *souq* was one of the places I loved to explore. An outdoor
marketplace full of spices, fabrics, tailoring shops, and gold,
the *souq* is a common gathering place in most Arabic countries.
City blocks are filled with shopkeepers vending beautiful smells,
colors, fabrics, textures, and tastes. The hot sidewalks are
exhilarating, and I came alive as I elbowed my way through the
constant crowds with the world chattering around me.

One entire area of the *souq* sells nothing but spices. Vendors
offer large bins of vibrant colored and odored spices you can buy
by the weight — saffron, ginger, cardamom, cinnamon, and, of
course, the ever-present curry. Rows and rows of recognizable as

well as exotic aromas—you can smell the spice *souq* from streets away. The humidity causes the collage of odors to commingle and become this most amazing sweet-and-spice. Like a perfume that reminds you of a certain someone the minute you catch even the slightest hint of the aroma, the spice *souq* stays in your memory.

The gold *souq* sells rose gold, white gold, 24-karat gold—every kind of gold imaginable—by the gram at a much cheaper price than you could ever find in the States. Extravagantly filigreed collars, oversized watches and rings, millions upon millions of bangle bracelets. The gold *souq* is filled with slick Middle Eastern salesmen and wide-eyed Americans looking for a deal. The bartering made me uncomfortable at first, but I came to enjoy it once I got good at it. Nothing had a "set price," so creative bargaining became a necessary survival skill.

In the fabric *souq*, shop front after shop front displays cottons, trims, shirting, wool, and embellished black silks for *abayas*. Tailoring shops rim the fabric storefronts, offering amazing deals for one-of-a-kind suits, shirts, dresses, and coats. If you wanted it, you could have it made. This was a creative challenge to me. One I took seriously. I purchased all sorts of trims and silks and shirting—all of which I had elaborate plans for: a duvet cover for our bed when we returned to the States, a dress for me, button-down shirts for Steve. The options and opportunities were endless.

Almond-stuffed dates. Battery-operated dancing camels. Alarm clocks in the shape of a mosque. Every kind of *abaya* and *thobe* you could want. Head scarves. Roadside stands selling heavenly *shawarmas*—a fresh piece of *naan* stuffed with lamb cut right off the spit and doused with yogurt sauce and a bit of

found art

hot sauce. I rarely left the *souq* without a *shawarma* or, at the very least, a fresh juice smoothie from the *shawarma* stand.

"A ja-ooooose?" The man behind the counter never forgets to ask.

"Bananas, oranges, strawberries," I always order the same thing for myself and something with mangoes for Steve.

The *shawarma* stand owner goes about chopping up the fresh fruit.

"*Shukran*," I tell the man as I hand him a couple of *dinars* for our entire lunch.

I like watching the storekeepers pull the metal grates down over their storefronts and turn a prayer rug toward Mecca for afternoon prayers. I peek through the window and watch them go off into another world of worship right there in the shop. Before my eyes, a rug salesman becomes a pilgrim and a rug shop holy ground.

The *souq* is the best of humanity—languages from all over the world layering on each other melodically, exotic creations at every turn, passionate sales pitches, gleaming gold, real and abundant life. The dirty pavement, steaming in the heat, emits beauty and color and odor and all of the things that make me feel awake in the world.

Though the blistering-hot months of August and September were in full swing, I traipsed through every square inch with my arms and legs (and everything in between) covered, as was expected of all American military personnel. I walked the entire *souq* more than once, staring and shopping and holding hands with Steve. I walked and walked as if I were looking for something and until I felt like this foreign world was finally inviting me in as one of its own.

Our favorite shop in all of the *souq* is Khazana, a Persian carpet store. We always ask for Yousef when we visit. A middle-aged man over six feet tall and pencil-thin, Yousef has graying hair and glasses and badly capped teeth. And we love him. The minute Yousef sees us coming, he gets the tea started.

We drink syrupy sweet tea from tiny painted shot-sized glasses as we perch on a pile of carpets. Yousef understands that looking at rugs is as much about the experience and appreciation of the artistry as it is about the purchase, so he always teaches us about the history of the designs, allows us to borrow a few to "try on" at home, and even encourages us to take our time in selecting a rug because, he says, "you will have for the rest of your life."

"You will pass on to your children and your children's children someday," he tells us. "Take your time. Make good selection."

He's taught us about the Tabriz fish design from Iran with its saturated colors and mesmerizing center medallion, the kind of rug a man would put in his study right underneath a leather chair—strong, rich, sophisticated. He's introduced us to the exquisitely expensive Qums made entirely of silk. They are to look at and not walk on, so they hang on the walls instead of sitting in piles on the floor. The sunlight plays tricks with their colors, enlivening the purple and aqua and silver patinas. Then the Gabbehs—one of Steve's favorites. Their wool is soft and inches thick, and their design is simple and childlike, with large blocks of colors and simple stick figure patterns. The tribal rugs from Afghanistan are thin and coarse and used for bedspreads and wall hangings as much as floor coverings.

I would like Yousef to be my friend. He is a very gentle, meek man, so different from many of the garish salesmen we've encountered. I've convinced myself that he genuinely cares for me — that he is after more than my money — seeing in me a kindred spirit, someone who appreciates his rugs as much as he does. Steve shares my feelings. We often stop by Khazana when he has a moment away from work. Part of Steve's therapy is flipping rugs, talking shop with Yousef, drinking tea.

The jewel of the Middle East, and therefore the *souq*, is the rugs. They perfectly typify the entire culture — opulent and yet entirely ancient. I found great, unexpected, soulful beauty in these rugs. Some of them were antiques, some more recently constructed, but none of them were completely new. Each one had a story — a region, a tribe, and a family that spent the better part of an entire year or more designing, dying the wool or silk, and weaving one solitary rug. Each one still had a bit of sand from Iran, Afghanistan, Turkmenistan, Uzbekistan, Turkey, Pakistan, or Tajikistan in its fringe.

Peace and breath were plenty in these moments with Yousef in the *souq*. Time slipped utterly away, as did any of the world's worries. We took our shoes off and pushed our bare toes down into the plush wool of the carpets as we would into sand on the beach. Sometimes we stretched out across a pile of rugs in the corner and talked and laughed as we ate our *shawarmas*. Sometimes we just listened as Yousef paraded a few of his most prized rugs in front of us, introducing them as if they were friends and telling us their stories.

Whether we stopped and flipped rugs, sifted our hands through a bin of bright red chili peppers, savored a bag of almond-stuffed dates, examined the yards of paper-thin silk, or paused just long enough to hear the thumping heartbeat of culture, I was aware, yet again, that beauty is not a luxury in life but a necessity. Beauty — certainly found in the eye of the beholder — possesses great power to heal.

Healing is the process of becoming whole where we once had gaping gashes or slivery fractures, or anything in between. I had all of the above, in different states of disrepair. Though the *souq* or the Gulf or Yousef or the silence weren't the cure in and of themselves, they were the spit and dirt that were mixed together and used as a salve on my badly blinded eyes.

I had been living in a dark place before all of this — a kind of darkness that creeps in very slowly and sinuously, and before I knew it, the lights had gone out in my soul. I had been walking around town like this for some time, living but not alive enough. The beauty of the world was lost on me, and all the things I loved were forgotten in lieu of all the things I thought I needed to be.

I couldn't remember what it felt like to create or rest, or what it felt like to breathe. I couldn't remember what it felt like to feel God, and I surely couldn't remember what it felt like to pray.

God has a way of taking the most unsuspecting elements and using them to bind us up. When the miracle happens, when he touches our eyes with these elements and we are able to see, we realize that even dirt and spit contain a beauty all their own.

I once visited a fabric shop in Los Angeles owned by a man who had escaped Iran during the Revolution. His wife was six months pregnant when they fled, the baby jumping inside her every time a bomb would detonate outside their house. They came to LA as refugees, bringing with them just a few vestiges of home. One of them was a beautiful rug the man had hanging in his shop.

"Where are you from?" I asked.

"Guess," he said.

"Somewhere near the Persian Gulf?" I answered.

"Iran," he said. "I'm impressed. Most people think Italian."

His response made me laugh. Then it made me recoil in annoyance. *Italian?* How would it feel to know most people in Los Angeles couldn't tell Italy from Iran if it were standing right in front of them? He had probably learned to laugh off this kind of ignorance, but the pain of it ran deeper and showed in his eyes when he began talking about his home in the glory days at the time of the Shah before the Revolution.

"Iran so beautiful in those days," he said.

He exhaled through his fingers as he shook his head back and forth slowly.

I waited for him to return to the fabric shop where we were both sitting, and he snapped back into the moment with a forceful "Now, not good," his words staccato and his head shaking faster.

The man and his wife left with little more than each other, somehow finding their way to Los Angeles, where they began to rebuild their lives alongside thousands of other Iranian refugees. This man's lifelong fate was maintaining, maybe even fighting for, a sense of his Iranian self amidst an alien country.

Part of maintaining his identity was the pride he took in his fabric shop. Maybe he didn't own a shop full of Persian rugs, but he had something. When I commented on the beauty and uniqueness of his fabric selections, he said, "Fabric like flower. All different. All beautiful."

Here is a man who, amid great pain, has managed to find some kind of joy and healing through the great beauty of his fabrics. Here is a man who, despite the prospect of living in a foreign place for the remainder of his life, has maintained his loves and his sense of self. In the face of the world's cruelty, he is more than a pitied victim. He has found art, and therefore healing, in the scraps and the threads.

After looking for the perfect rug, we purchased a Tabriz fish at Khazana. Yousef assured us we made a good selection. He even allowed us to take it to our flat for a couple of days to make sure the rug was right for us. Steve and I both agreed it was "the one."

Every time I look at that captivating center medallion, I remember Yousef and the *souq* and the syrupy sweet tea and the way it feels to really see. The light was just a flicker at first. That's how the healing begins — a faint but fervent flicker.

an original poem

8

gathering

When I was in junior high, I wrote tragically brooding poems about my family and horses. I read my creations to my friends, and all of us would cry. Sometimes I'd mention God simply because that would make the poems more pitiful and my friends more sympathetic. Anything to get a tear.

At that time, I was a thirteen-year-old girl, struggling in new ways with my parents' divorce. The divorce was four years old by then, but I was just beginning to understand what it meant to me. Looking back, I was probably angry, and the poetry served as a safe place to release my closeted anger in the form of injured quarter horses and unbroken Clydesdales. I was an unapologetic artist in those days, drumming up melancholy verse with gusto and ownership.

In college, I harkened back to my roots and took a poetry class from a woman who resembled a hobbit in most every way — a good and kindly hobbit, but a hobbit nonetheless. She epitomized nothing poetic, but she got us writing and expressing, and there is something to be said for getting adrenalized college students to sit down and get their inside world out on paper.

My college poems, like those of the junior high years, were

filled with affectations and effort, heavy-handed attempts at capturing this earth-altering voice that was sure to leave my professor moved, in awe of my work unequalled in all her years of teaching. No such luck.

The luck, I found through pure accident, was in the creating itself. The process of composing and capturing life mattered far more than the actual product. I basked in the extravagant pleasure of gathering and ordering words, each draft an inexhaustible, melancholic celebration of unrequited love or unparalleled friendship — or the very few other topics on a young coed's mind.

And then I got to graduate school.

Mark Twain once wrote about this exact thing. He loved the river, and so he set out to become a steamboat pilot and learn about all things river. But once he did, the romance drained right out. Instead of seeing the moon against the water, he saw the dangers in the changing tide. Beauty had become something to master, and he wondered aloud in an essay on the subject if he was better or worse off for learning his craft.

One listen to the MFA students' creative writing, and my poetry career careened into oblivion. Poetry, I learned, was a discipline for those with something seriously important to say.

Like Adam and Eve, who had once been walking through the garden as naked as jaybirds without any notion they were bare, I was all of a sudden painfully, embarrassingly aware of my nakedness. The voice of shame outfoxed me once again, reminding me that if I couldn't create something perfect, I'd better not create anything at all. I quickly grabbed all the animal skins and fig leaves I could find and covered up my most private parts.

For five years, I didn't write a single poem. Not even a

birthday limerick. What was the point? I couldn't well construct the epic archetypes and subversive activism my classmates managed to infuse into their masterpieces. Anything less would be pure drivel, I was convinced, and I lost the bit of truth that had been with me since junior high: art for art's sake.

Perfectionism is the archnemesis of creativity. Shame, too. The big-me poet of yesteryear, the fledgling artist who flung her soul headlong into expression, clammed up. That beautiful, unapologetic voice became suddenly self-conscious, and I silenced a profoundly important piece of me.

Until Bahrain.

The world was speaking to me, as it had always been, but I was finally in a place in which I could participate in the dialogue. All of a sudden, so many things needed to be recorded and connected. Material was limitless — a funny old man sleeping in his wheelbarrow out in front of the meat market exposing a mouth of badly compromised teeth, a woman swimming (or more accurately thrashing) in the Gulf wearing her full *abaya*, the feeling of being absolutely lost in newlywed love. I jotted notes constantly — on paper bags from Mega Mart, on napkins from the base food court, on the back of the chapel worship bulletin. All the stuff inside me came leaking out just as all the stuff outside me began seeping in.

One day, I even wrote a poem. Actually I scribbled in the margins of a notebook as if I couldn't help but get it down, as if it were the most natural thing to do, as if it were spilling out of me and couldn't even be contained by the lines on the page. Funny how life comes alive and gains accessibility right about the time we let go of needing to control the outcome, of needing things to be just so. I let my poem be spontaneously bad and overwritten, which was cause for celebration in and of itself.

When something really profound happened in the Old Testament, during the children-of-Israel-still-wandering times, the Israelites memorialized the event by gathering stones. They called them "stones of remembrance," a reminder of the greatness of the great event. The point of these stones was to commemorate what God had done — rescued them from impending destruction, mounting stupidity, wrong turns, and other general lapses in judgment. I assume this practice was necessary because they, like me, were quick to forget what was really important.

In one mind-blowing example, God alters the flow of the Jordan River so his people can cross to safety. Joshua orders twelve men to each gather one stone from the riverbed and place all of them together to serve as a sign, a memorial, that God had intervened against all odds.

I have a hunch that the practice of gathering and stacking the stones was as much about the children of Israel as it was about God. These stones were reminders to wake up and see what is possible in the world, to notice the miracles, to even participate in a miraculous event now and then — to stop worrying and making excuses and apologizing and "should"ing and sniveling, and instead simply believe. Step into the current and see what happens. Get your feet wet instead of paralytically wondering how cold the water might feel or how strong the pull might be or how on earth you're going to explain that you haven't shaved your legs or gotten a pedicure for such an occasion.

Somehow, in Bahrain, I rediscovered the nerve to believe that my truest self mattered, that my thoughts counted, that art for art's sake was indeed a valid use of my time — whether or not things came out perfectly (cuz, news flash, they're never gonna).

I still have the notebook where that poem is scribbled in the corner. The few lines aren't anything special. They look more like an afterthought or a doodle or a grocery list you'd start making when you're supposed to be listening in church. But that's not the point.

The point, and again I happened on to this by accident, was that for one moment, I was willing to strip all the way down to my true self and listen and look for God in my world. And now I have a few tiny stones — some slivered chips and pebbles and rocks — gathered and stacked so that I will never forget.

There, in that little notebook, is something far more important than paper and binding and scrawling verse. There, in that little notebook, is me. Recorded. Rediscovered. Reclaimed.

Nice to meet you again.

building up

My friend Tina gave me a greeting card with a woman on the front who looked kind of like Mona Lisa in the face but had an enormous amount of red hair jutting out in every direction like a frizzy fire. The inside of the card read, "Nobody noticed her ankles."

I kept this card in plain sight for years as a reminder to be a bit gentler with myself when it comes to the parts of my body I am particularly unfond of, the ankles being high on the list. The card also speaks to the power of assets — how one glorious feature (eccentric, beautiful, or otherwise) can cover a multitude of sins. I've always said that a good accessory can do wonders. Most important, the card makes the self-obsessions I take so seriously and waste so much time worrying about seem just a bit absurd.

After a few months in Bahrain, I set out looking for a job in my field. That is, the field I have received degrees, training, and professional experience in. Happily, I was hired to teach English classes in the university extension program on base. Active-duty personnel could finish their degrees, one or two classes at a time, while they worked their military jobs. An application, a brief interview, a review of my CV—and I was hired to teach basic composition.

As the time approached for the class to begin, I received a phone call that enrollment was low and they were going to postpone the class until next term. No problem. We agreed I would wait until then to begin. But the next session didn't make enrollment either. In fact, the entire time I lived in Bahrain, not a single class materialized.

I took a hint and decided that, for some reason, I was to spend my time in Bahrain doing things other than what I was trained, licensed, and had been paid in the past to do. I took up two jobs of a totally different persuasion. These two jobs are not the kind you sign up for because you should, because you have experience doing them, or because they would look good on your résumé. Quite the opposite actually. Something much different must compel you.

The first—and undoubtedly the more dubious of the two— was bagging in the Ship Store (the name of the mini grocery store on base). A couple of other Navy wives who were looking for some quick cash roped me into becoming a bagger. There was no formal training for the job, just some broad brushstrokes from the cashier such as "watch the eggs," "cold with cold," "double bag the milk," and a few other handy reminders—we worked for tips only, for example.

Every time someone came through the line, I bagged their groceries in exchange for some change or a dollar or two—depending on the size of their purchase. Shifts were typically about three hours long and commonly yielded a wad of cash at the end.

I've never had a job where I made a lot of money. Ever. I've worked as a teacher, for a nonprofit organization, and for a church. There's no money in any of that. But bagging — now that's a different story.

The best part of my day was coming home and counting up all my bagging money. First, I organized everything into piles — ones, fives, quarters, dimes — and then I started counting. I kept my earnings in a jar in our room and dipped into my savings now and then when I wanted to treat myself to something special. I tried to keep Steve in the dark on the actual total in the jar so he wouldn't expect me to pull my own weight in the household. Bagging money, I made clear to him, was not for groceries or gas. My hard-earned tips were for far more important things such as trips to the M.A.C. store in the Seef Mall and online shopping for aerobics outfits — which provides, incidentally, a perfect segue to my other Bahraini job.

In addition to my bagging job, I became certified to teach aerobics. Again, I never set out to teach aerobics, but when the call came, I answered. I heard a rumor on the streets that the class coordinators were looking for new instructors. I signed up for the weekend training and soon found myself in front of a class with a Britney mic, a boom box, and a pink step.

While it's surely tempting to make some immediate and potentially derogatory assumptions about me based on the above information, allow me to clarify some things.

I didn't teach Fancy Aerobics. I couldn't really do compli-cated steps or those long combinations that some of the other instructors were good at. They danced around like puppets on a string, singing into the microphone. I lumbered and gasped. Mine was more Jock Aerobics.

I played competitive volleyball from the time I was in the

seventh grade until I graduated from college. All of the children in my family went to college on an athletic scholarship — my older sister and I both played volleyball, and my younger brother played football and baseball. Athletics has played at least some part in just about every family memory I have. Volleyball went far beyond a sport in my life to practically becoming another person — a co-parent, an accountability partner, a companion, a therapist, a cheerleader, a god, even the closest thing I had to a boyfriend at times.

My athletic career kept me on the straight and narrow when my faith wasn't strong enough to keep me there. I stayed away from drugs, partying, sex, and starvation, not because God had encouraged me to keep away from such interests, but because of the fear of what I could lose on the volleyball court.

The other thing volleyball gave me was an acceptance of my body when, at any other moment, the big hands and feet, broad shoulders, man-calves, and tree-trunk quads were a source of personal contention. On the volleyball court, I needed my body and — dare I say — loved it. Or, at the very least, I loved what my body could do. During a match, I forgave my ankles for being thick, my build for being "athletic," my height for being tallish. I saw the purpose for such additions to my genetic makeup. In my own way, I said thank you to the skin and bones and muscles when on all other occasions I was likely to be critical.

Then I had to go and grow up. I had to leave Volleyball Never-Never Land behind for more adult things such as master's degrees, employment, and running on treadmills. Ironically, around that time I also began a much more adversarial relationship with my body. I didn't so much abuse it physically as I did emotionally. I reprimanded and demanded and generally apologized on behalf of it, and where we had once been partners, we were now no longer on speaking terms.

That's where teaching Jock Aerobics comes in. I took all my years of volleyball, weight training, and stretching, and I made a class out of what I knew to do. Shockingly, people came. The women came because of the ungodly amount of lunges I made us all do (women will show up to anything that makes their butts sore). The men came because of the ungodly amount of abs I made us all do (men will show up to anything that makes their abs sore).

Most of the people who attended my classes did not have good bodies. That's why they were there. They needed encouragement and care and someone to push them just a wee bit. They needed a sense of accomplishment in an area of their lives where they were all pretty discouraged. I've been there.

We worked hard together and celebrated what each of us could do well (because not everyone could do everything well, but everyone could do something well). We focused on assets instead of always belaboring liabilities. I began to remember the things about my body I had once appreciated — the muscles and strength and durability — and I began to appreciate them again. Jock Aerobics turned into body-building-up.

Teaching aerobics on base was not lucrative, not nearly as lucrative as bagging, but the sweating was good for mind, body, and soul. The spiritual discipline of perspiration released the toxins in my spirit and gave me new eyes for what I saw in the mirror.

Bodybuilding takes much more courage than body hating. That's why it's so hard. In teaching aerobics, I stumbled on to

found art

a piece of myself that had been long lost in the fury of being a grown-up. Instead of teaching composition — a perfectly respectable and responsible use of my time — I somehow found myself teaching aerobics to a steamy roomful of sweaty military personnel.

And guess what — nobody noticed my ankles. Not even me.

10
laughing

After we had lived in Capital Centre for a couple of months, we decided to move. Leaving our first home was both triumphant and tragic, really. I loved Capital Centre in the way you love a dorm room — not because you want to live there the rest of your life but because it has offered solace to you during one of the most important transitions.

We contacted Jasmine, a Turkish, non-Muslim realtor, who helped Steve secure Capital Centre. She agreed to help us find our next residence.

Capital Centre was a fifteen-minute car drive, each way, to the base. Our lives would become much simpler if Steve was able to ride his bike back and forth from home to work and if I could drop in on a moment's notice when he had a break in the day. The move enabled us to spend more time together. A relocation also enabled us to move into one of the brand-new flats that sat on a land reclamation project just a mile or so outside the base gate. Jasmine scouted out this particular building and reported back that, though the construction was not quite complete (a scary thing in Bahrain because it's hard to nail anyone down on such minor details as, "When will it be finished?"), the flat was going to be fabulous.

Jasmine and I drove around in her car on our way to look at the new building as well as some others in the surrounding area of Juffair. Jasmine was just a few years older than I, though I had to believe she looked *far* older. During the car ride from Capital Centre to Juffair, I learned she had a young son and no husband, a very rare situation in that neck of the woods.

Let me also add that Jasmine smelled intensely of cigarettes, perfume, and body odor all at the same time—an entrancing aroma. She wore thick foundation and heavy lipstick, and her face always looked seconds away from melting right off the front of her head. I liked her for all these reasons.

The foundation for the new building we were visiting had been carved right out of the sand, with little thought put toward a way to actually access the high-rise, so we traversed the quarter mile of unpaved road in Jasmine's tiny car.

The road system in Bahrain is much like the trash system and the mail system—nonexistent. A system *does* exist, albeit convoluted, for phone and Internet services, which are clearly the country's main priorities. No paved roads. Men dressed as shepherds. But everyone, and I mean everyone (except the Navy personnel and the poor Shi'as), has a Mercedes and a cell phone.

"Any plans on putting in a road?" I ask optimistically, as my head hits the ceiling of Jasmine's car and the fillings in my teeth begin to feel as though they're being pulled out by magnets.

Jasmine furrows her brow and turns her mouth down as she shakes her head no—as if to say, "There is no need for road here, silly American girl."

The building is called Starview. Of course, no sign displaying the word *Starview* actually exists. (The signage system in Bahrain is, apparently, much like the road system, the trash system, and the mail system.) Jasmine was tipped off by the receptionist, Mohammed, an effeminate man with bad skin and an overly zealous stare. He pointed to the star on top of the building when he told her the name. His contemptuous look seemed to communicate our ineptness for not agreeing that the star completely spoke for itself.

In a way, it did. A huge techno-colored, three-dimensional star sat on top of the building like a candle on a birthday cake. At night, the star exploded into a thousand neon colors. I found the whole presentation a tad tacky. Mohammed clearly considered it heaven.

Starview was set right beside the Gulf, but certainly not the same Gulf I'd become accustomed to sharing with Richard from the BBC. This Gulf was not nearly as sexy. The coastline had been messed with from all the land reclamation, and the shore was littered and shallow and dotted with abandoned *dhows* rotting in the heat. The Starview Gulf looked more like a stagnant bay than an ocean. I would have to sacrifice my previously perfect view of the water and the palms and the *corniche* where *thobes* and *abayas* strolled, but in exchange I would get to enjoy brand-new furniture, a huge-screen television, two maids, a workout room (where I could practice my aerobics routines), and a pool. Starview also had a Nepalese watchman. That alone I considered a sign.

Because the building construction was still being finished, only a couple of flats were ready enough to show. Of course, none of them were on the ground floor. And, *of course*, the elevator and the air-conditioning were the last things to be installed in the building.

Jasmine and I headed to the stairwell, where a pleasant 130-degree heat greeted us. We had been given the key to Flat 41 (on the fourth floor), and the climb was absolutely insipid.

Jasmine was about to melt away as she wheezed up the stairs, swearing with every step that she would quit smoking the minute we get back to the car.

Thankfully, the flat was worth the climb. Flat 41 was to be our new home, and I knew this instantly. Floor-to-ceiling windows made the already sky-high ceilings look taller as light flooded into the main living room/dining room combination. Every room was furnished, and the kitchen was stocked. The master bedroom even came equipped with a purple-velvet chaise where one could lounge and look out to the water if so desired.

I was checking out the kitchen when Jasmine called to me from the master bedroom.

"Do you have king-sized shits?" she yelled.

"Excuse me?" I called back, immediately walking toward the master bedroom.

"Do you have king-sized shits?" she yelled out again, this time louder.

I walked into the doorway of the bedroom and looked straight at Jasmine without saying a word, realizing that she was as serious as a heart attack.

"This bed will need king-sized shits," she said, pointing to the king-sized bed in the middle of the room.

(*Oooh. Sheeeeeets*, I think to myself. *She's saying sheets.*)

"Yes. Yes, I think we do," I said.

Steve and I later met with the owner/landlord/sole financier, Mr. Sharif, to review the lease and secure Flat 41, which, we were told, would be ready for us to move into just a couple of weeks later — *Insha'Allah.*

After meeting Mr. Sharif, I better understood why the flat

came with the hugest TV I had ever seen, as well as a purple-velvet chaise in the master bedroom. He was extraordinarily wealthy, and he liked everyone to know it. He also let us know he was celebrating his marriage to a third wife and continued to build buildings so he would have somewhere to house them all. He thought this was hysterical. I let the corners of my mouth turn up almost imperceptibly as I glared at Steve, just to make it perfectly clear that any acknowledgment of such "humor" would not end well for him.

Mr. Sharif handed us the lease paperwork, and I was not at all surprised to see a way-too-big headshot of himself cut and pasted next to a Bahraini flag at the top of every page. Starview's receptionist, Mohammed, flitted around Mr. Sharif—stapling papers and staring—as if he were going to come out of his skin with reverence and awe. Mohammed took a liking to Steve and asked him all sorts of questions about his job at the base, which Steve found suspect and inappropriate and took immediate offense to.

"Ohhh, fine sir, do you work on the base?" Mohammed asked Steve, eying a pile of uniforms we had just picked up from the dry cleaner.

"No," Steve replied flatly and without expression, acting as though Mohammed were some sort of spy. We both knew full well Mohammed lacked many of the qualities required to pull off anything resembling a terrorist conspiracy. He was an overeager twentysomething who would have jumped in Steve's pocket had Steve let him. Steve, in his Steve way, was having none of it.

So began the standoff between Mohammed and Steve. The more Steve froze him out, the more Mohammed gushed. I just stood back and watched the whole awkward two-step—Steve becoming increasingly hostile, and Mohammed becoming increasingly adoring—and laughed.

When we got the word that Flat 41 was finished—only a couple weeks later than promised—we hired a Pakistani moving crew and a rattletrap moving truck. We loaded a random assortment of belongings, including quite a few leftovers from Steve's bachelor days (the stuffed head of an impala and a blessbuck, for example), and we headed to Starview. On our way to the new building, I drove behind the moving truck as it rolled up on two wheels around every single roundabout, Pakistani movers hanging off every side.

What a country.

One of Starview's great luxuries was its closer proximity to my newest friend, Maryann. I didn't have many friends in Bahrain, but the friends I made were memorable, as all real friends should be. Richard, the BBC reporter, I soon considered a friend, or, at the very least, a companion to my quiet days inside the walls of Capital Centre. Yousef, the rug salesman from Khazana, held a special place in my heart and seemed to become the reason—as much as the stunning rugs—we visited his shop in the *souq*. Then came the very small handful of Navy wives I began to run with. Among my favorites was Maryann.

Maryann was a day-drinking Catholic about ten years my senior, whom I was introduced to at the food court on base because our husbands worked together. Her husband was perpetually deployed, and her four-year-old son was perpetually potty training. I tried to be of some encouragement to her on both accounts, but I can't say I blamed her for edging off her foul mood with a glass or four of Chardonnay every once in a while.

I loved Maryann most for the self-proclaimed "big footprint" she left wherever she went. She loved and spoke loudly, which reminded me of my own family, and she immediately embraced me with verve and vigor and would not let me go.

Maryann loved her son as Rizpah of the Old Testament loved hers—with the loyalty, vigilance, and ferocity of a cornered mama bear. But, as any true love is able to do, he could spin her up like a top. I specifically remember a scene in Al Jazeera grocery store when they were pitted against each other, locked in combat on either side of a grocery cart, with every Bahraini woman in the store staring at them from behind her veil. In the next moment, they were laughing out loud as they loaded groceries into the car. This, again, took me right back to my growing-up days and the combustible push-pull I shared with my own mother.

A few times a week, I'd go over to Maryann's beautifully enormous villa out in Busaiteen, on the north side of the island—"over the sail bridge and right past the petrol pumps," as she always said when she gave directions to her home. Invariably, she'd be scrubbing up a long-forgotten "deposit" from her son in the corner of the fourth-story playroom, cursing and seething with every scrub. She'd relay the story to me—how she came across the said "offering," which choice words she bellowed, how royally miffed she was, how she didn't go to an expensive university to be alone in the Middle East scrubbing up feces, and on and on.

She'd open a bottle (if one was not open already) and continue sharing her son's latest anal-retentive strategy to keep from having to go when and where he was supposed to. She'd recount the various "surprises" he would leave for her throughout the nooks and crannies and corners of their

found art

6,000-square-foot villa. After a long venting, she'd come up for air.

In that dramatic pause, the wind would often shift, and a slight smile would creep across her face as she gained a little perspective. Then we would both laugh, sometimes until we cried. What else could you do? We lived in a pressure cooker with intensity around every corner. I think we were each other's therapy that year, providing respite and levity in the midst of a world of heaviness.

Rare and sacred are the moments when the most organic gift appears—though it may leave as quickly as it comes—that interrupts the darkness all around it. The world may be falling apart, may be at war even, but the sound of laughter can be heard from one small corner as it spills out and fills in the deepest grooves of sadness.

Laugh with those who laugh, the book of Romans says. Laugh while we have the time and reason and opportunity, for the world is far too full of king-sized ... well, you get the idea.

a bit of basting thread

11

tearing

Steve and I settled into a rhythm in the new flat. He rode his bike to the base, so I didn't have to get up at such an ungodly hour to get him to work. This was helpful because my day revolved less around having to transport and wait for him. Instead, my day revolved almost entirely around me, which was, of course, far more convenient.

With each week, I became more accustomed to him. I started learning his signals and signs and moods and tones. I started picking up on more of the undercurrents that make him who he is. Learning to be married to someone is like trying to learn the habits of a new roommate, the needs of a new baby, and the creaky floorboards of a new house, all at the same time. Truthfully, I entered our first year of marriage with very low expectations. I just assumed we'd be tolerating each other most of the time, and when we weren't doing that, we'd be hopelessly confronted with the dark reality of the person we had actually married. Sounds super-romantic when I put it that way.

After all, I tried to comfort myself, we hardly knew each other. What we *did* know of each other could fill encyclopedia volumes compared to the amount of time we'd spent together.

A few weeks here and there was the sum total of our face time. I'd seen the neighborhood barista more frequently.

Our first few months of marriage were about understanding each other and ourselves too. As soon as I made sense of my own stirrings and resistances, he'd gone and jumped to another song altogether, and I had to figure out how I was going to keep in step with him and the new tune. That is marriage. Learning the dance. A few months into the blessed union, I was just trying to get the steps down and yet not try so hard that I lost my ear for the beauty of the music. The entire endeavor is a resiliently delicate thing.

Starview was witness to our first major blowup. Early one morning we had discussed our plans for the day. The way the afternoon unfolded was not what we had agreed on. I came home later than I had anticipated, and Steve was angry. The general gist of the argument has become the subject matter for much of what we fight about in our marriage. This rub is the signature fight at the root of many other fights — the battle we come back to over and over again.

Certain dynamics in a marriage are set very early on. A very specific culture — a way of doing things, resolving things, talking about things, fighting about things — is created from the very beginning. Nothing short of divine intervention and extensive therapy can undo what that early culture does.

The minute I feel controlled in the slightest, I turn into Raging Crazy Person. The minute "the other party" feels misled, he turns into Unreasonable Expectations Person (my perception, not his, of course). I feel controlled; he feels manipulated. I cry for grace; he cries for fairness. I resent his "no" to me; he resents my "yes" to the world. We are quickly reduced to our own entrenched ways of seeing things.

On the maiden voyage of this well-worn fight, the understanding man I loved turned into someone impossible to reason with, a man who simply found profound pleasure in keeping me under his thumb. The loving and accommodating wife I had been up to that moment got one whiff of control issues in the air and became belligerent and wild.

As much as we'd all like marriage to wipe the slate clean, it only serves to illuminate, not eliminate, what has already been etched in stone. I've learned this from experience. My issues with Steve found their deep roots in the already-spoken-of previous relationship where I had felt parented and patronized at every turn. Maybe I was just a wee bit oversensitive to such dynamics happening again, afraid of finding out that Steve was every bit as unreasonable as Bad Boyfriend had been. Of course none of Steve's "big feelings" had any baggage behind them whatsoever. It took us about a year and a half of counseling to figure out some of this. Good for us.

By the time the whole fight had finished, I was a dripping puddle of tears, sure that our relationship would never be the same again. In fact, the thought even crossed my mind that I should consider returning home to San Diego, as things had clearly and irrevocably changed between us. I had married an unreasonably angry person. And he had married a boundaryless, shameful one. *Surprise!*

I stayed in our room and cried on our bed while Steve cooled off in the other room. I began my very own midfight ritual (one I still practice to this day): I rehearsed my injuries and rehearsed his injustices and wept deep, heaving sobs until I finally came to the harsh conclusion that a huge, unsightly gash had been ripped right down the middle of our relationship — and there wasn't enough superglue or thread or staples or Velcro to put things back together again.

Finally, Steve came into our bedroom and sat on the bed next to me, a different man from the one who had left the room twenty minutes ago. This, again, has become part of our marriage culture. Steve is almost always the one to come to me. From the very beginning, he has been the one to seek restoration first. I thank God for that, because often I don't have the maturity to seek him out. I hide in another room and snivel and whimper, always wishing simultaneously he would come to me and he would move out. In the moment, I often want to punish him more than I want to reconcile. He is not nearly this juvenile. He will leave the room for a bit, but he always comes back, wielding a soft tone and kind words.

The night of our first fight, he did what he would continue to do for years to come. He came back to me. Though he had sought me out, I wouldn't even pick up my buried head and look at him.

"Babe, I'm sorry," he said as he put his hand on my leg. I unburied my face from the bed just long enough to show him how frothing and oozing and generally terrible looking I was. I wanted him to see how utterly undone our fight had made me feel. I wanted him to see the damage he had caused, and I wanted him to know I might not forgive him.

"It's going to be OK," he said calmly. I wanted to believe him, but I didn't know if I could trust him. I didn't know if I had made him so mad that he would never be able to love me again. I didn't know if I wanted to love him anymore. I didn't know if I could fight like that with someone and then truly make up and move on. It didn't seem possible.

found art

I cried a little more until I finally said the truest thing I could think to say: "I'm scared."

My anger was undoubtedly trumped by fear. When I admitted what I was really feeling—to him and to myself—the torrent of tears started all over again.

"I know you are. We're going to be OK." His voice was low and calming, and he kept his hand on my leg. "It's a fight. That's all it is. We're going to be fine."

I picked myself up off the bed and sobbed on his shoulder a while longer, just feeling thankful we didn't have to part ways so early into things. The flight home alone would have been a beast. Plus, my mom had already told him, "Steve, you can't bring her back." So that was that.

After a few moments in his arms, he said in his Steve way, "Do you want Chinese for dinner?" and I knew he had moved on. I, on the other hand, was still hiccuping and breathless, unsure if we would really be able to bounce back from such a trauma.

The Chinese takeout arrived, and we watched TV on the couch. Just being close to him was good. I started to relax a bit and allow things to normalize. I tried to forgive him, even though forgiving felt like the hardest thing to do, and I tried to forgive myself for becoming so crazed. After a few hours, I finally came to the conclusion that we had survived our first real fight, and nothing had been broken too badly.

A few hours later, we said good night, and I lay awake next to a very sleeping Steve. I wandered into the bathroom of Flat 41, closed the huge wooden door, sat down on the edge of the bidet basin, and began to cry again. The bathroom is where I always go to cry. The cool floor and total darkness create a safe sanctuary where I can become heaving and guttural without an audience.

Within moments, my face was in my hands, and I was muffling sobs. Pain came out of nowhere and out of everywhere. Pain piled on pain. I just kept crying it out like sweat through my pores. Every layer giving way to another.

Pain is gawky and ungainly and never ties up neatly. It hangs on like an old infirm dog that needs to be put down. For all these reasons, I hate sitting in the discomfort. I hate the way hurting makes me feel out of control and weak.

I want to be the kind of person who is unmoved by my own suffering, who is unaffected by the things that reduce most people. I've always carried the misguided thought that the strong people are those who could experience something really difficult and come out of it unfazed. These are the people who teach the world how to cope.

I resisted the invitation that was hanging in the air because I didn't want to acknowledge the pain I was feeling. Deep down, I knew the source, but I didn't want to go where I knew I needed to go. What I was feeling had little to do with the rift between Steve and me earlier in the evening. The pain was shooting up from a much deeper tear, and I didn't want to go near it. This tear is jagged and raw, and the scar reopens from time to time because it's the kind of wound that is so very difficult to heal once and for all.

12

mending

Sitting on the edge of the bidet in the master bathroom, with the Middle Eastern winds, sands, and waters keeping me company, I let myself slip down into the core of my own soul. I didn't fast-rope down. I eased, painstakingly, until I could feel the thing I had reluctantly come into the bathroom to feel in the first place.

My parents divorced the year I was in the fourth grade. Every week, Mr. Meridian, my fourth-grade teacher, would catch up to me as I was walking the long walk to the pickup line after school. I would spot Miss Royce, my neighbor and carpool driver, in the long line of cars, and I'd head toward her as fast as I could, trying to blend into the sea of other students. But somehow Mr. Meridian would still manage to ambush me.

"Leeana, are you doing OK?" he'd ask, with his head turned, looking at me while we walked. Since he and I were just about the same height, his chocolate-milk eyes would lock on to mine if I ever looked over at him.

"Oh yeah, I'm fine. Good," I would say nervously, trying to be cool like an adult but feeling embarrassed like a child. The modest shorts I wore under my Christian-school-length skirt chafed my legs as I tried to push the pace toward the car, thinking I might still be able to lose him if I walked fast enough. My heart beat hard and my stomach burned from the footrace and unwanted attention. But he was persistent.

"OK, but you know you can always talk to me if you ever need to. You can come find me after school or at recess, and we can just talk if there's anything you need to tell me," he would say.

"I know. I'm OK." I'd manage a convincing smile.

That was our game of chase every week. He'd hunt me down on my way to the pickup line and ask me how I was doing, and I would feel flushed and nauseated and desperate to dive into the backseat of Miss Royce's blue sedan and yell "Go, go, go!" like a bank robber ducking into a getaway car.

I never knew if my mom asked him to keep an eye on me that year, or if he took a special interest in me because he heard from another source what was going on in my house. Maybe he saw something in my eyes, an uncharacteristic heaviness that even I was unaware of.

I could have no sooner verbalized whatever was going on inside me than I could have outrun him to the pickup line. I had no words for what was happening at home. Absolutely none. I would hear my older sister Laura crying in the shower. I would hear my mom crying in her closet. But the pain I witnessed made me feel awkward and uncomfortable, like my entire life was taking place atop eggshells, and no matter where I walked I was in danger of cracking something very fragile. This pushed the words deeper into me instead of giving them space to come out.

It never occurred to me that I should tell Mr. Meridian I was having a hard time watching my mom and my sister in so much pain. It simply never occurred to me that *I* was in pain. All I felt was lost. And the words were lost within me.

My parents married fairly young. My mom was right out of college, my dad right out of graduate school. They came to San Diego to pursue more education, and five years later, they had Laura. Five more years, and I was born, and Trey followed two years after that. My parents went about the tasks of raising a family, connecting to a church, and developing careers—my mom teaching part-time and my dad guiding a local Christian college through accreditation before becoming president. Just one year after he was named president, things changed.

The college was located on the same campus as our church and my sister's high school, so when it became public that my parents were divorcing, the news was just that. Public. My dad resigned from his position and moved out of our house. My mom scrambled to find a full-time job teaching at a junior high.

I vaguely remember my dad moving into an apartment near Trey's Little League field, though I never visited him there. Sometimes he'd walk over to the field during one of Trey's games, and I never knew exactly what to do. Should I leave my mom's side and go to him, or should I stay with her? I didn't want things to be uncomfortable, but they always were.

As all three of us kids grew up and got involved in athletics, much of our family time was spent at sporting events—my mom in one area of the bleachers, my dad in another. About halfway through the game, I'd go sit with him before returning to my mom at some later point, seesawing back and forth between two parents. The games were a microcosm of the acute tension of life. Holidays, weddings, graduations—being with one parent meant leaving the other.

The child inside me still feels that raw tension. Even though

I know life is complicated and involves difficult situations that require sensitivity and graciousness, the child in me feels punished often, drowning beneath the constant threat of letting a parent down. Part of me still believes that loving one parent will alienate the other.

"There is nothing human beings share more intensely than childhood," I heard Carlos Eire, a Cuban refugee, say at a lecture. We all share a time when life is open to us, and we take it in with the naïveté of youth. Childhood can come to a halt through any number of means—the dramatic and the subtle—all equally devastating. After all, what happens in our early years are the things we take with us into every year after. And that makes childhood fertile soil for pain.

Today, having divorced parents is as common as having cable. This doesn't make divorce any less difficult. If anything, it makes it more so. The child of divorce can feel like her parents' breakup is no big deal—that everyone deals with such inconveniences and that she better get over it and get on with life.

Judaism has many traditions associated with bereavement. One common ritual involves the rending, or tearing, of garments after receiving the news of a deceased loved one. Tearing the clothing recklessly, in a place other than a seam, is an outward expression of inward grief and a signal to others that you are in a period of mourning.

The tearing of garments is rich with meaning. Far from a haphazard exercise, rending is a practice with unique guidelines for every loss. Traditionally, grieving parents tear their clothing directly over the heart. The other relatives of the deceased rend their clothing as well, but the heart tear is reserved for the parents alone, as if their heart is literally ripped open by the loss of their child.

A special tradition also exists for children who have lost a parent. During the week following the funeral, if a child of the deceased needs to change his or her clothes, he or she must tear the clothes before removing them. None of the other family members are required to do this. Sons and daughters may then baste, or temporarily stitch, their clothing back together if that set of clothing is needed for a function or holiday. But they are never allowed to permanently sew these clothes back together again. The wound that remains after losing a parent may heal, but the visible scars on their clothing will serve as a reminder of the scar that remains in their lives forever.

What would it be like to live in a place where the rending of garments is practiced? What would it be like to walk by a bereft young mother whose outer coat had a jagged rip over her heart? What if you were standing in line at the grocery store beside someone whose shirt was temporarily stitched together with big basting stitches?

We hide our losses well, usually coping with adequate resilience. But what if we were allowed to wear our scars? What if we gave ourselves permission to acknowledge our pain?

Some days, I still find myself confused by the events of my childhood. Divorce is a strange thing. After the divorce, my dad married Becky, a kind and loving woman who is now a part of our family. My dad and Becky have been married longer than my parents were married. The dynamics have, in many ways, become our normal now. But once in a while, I try to think back to the days when my parents were married and we all lived in one house together. I can hardly remember that such a time existed. What sticks out more clearly is the long walk from my fourth-grade classroom to the pickup line, and Mr. Meridian shadowing me the entire time.

Losing a parent—whether to divorce, death, jail, drugs, alcohol, depression, busyness, anger, abuse, physical illness, or religion—scars us indelibly.

There in the bathroom, I was wearing my pain like a torn garment. For the first time, I was a wife—and I understood the unique gift of having a husband. I understood the feeling of having something with someone that is important and lasting. I also understood, in my own small way, what it feels like when that something has been threatened.

I grieved the loss of my parents' marriage on an entirely new level—not only as the child who lost out but as the adult who could see what was at stake. The fight with Steve was still fresh, and I realized how frightening and tragic it must have been to feel your marriage slipping through your fingers.

All these years later, we are all still stumbling some days, managing others, and thriving some too. Putting things back together is never easy; that's why mending is such a sacred act. As evidenced by my reluctance with Steve, I'm not good at this kind of magic on my own. I am defensive and proud and—more than anything—scared. I'm quick to punish (others and myself) because I'm often so afraid of getting hurt or getting hurt again. All of these things and more make me a bad candidate for forgiving and forgetting.

I want to be the one who will thread the needle, no matter how difficult, and begin stitching, but I need help to actually get started. Desperately. Restoration requires a miracle, and I know of only one miracle worker.

13

letting go

A few years after my parents were married, they bought a house in El Cajon on the eastern side of San Diego County. Laura was a toddler when they purchased the home, and Trey and I were both born there.

After they divorced, the house went to my mom, and she has lived in the yellow stucco four-bedroom ever since. A lot of life has been lived in that house. Maybe even more than one person should have to live.

In a handful of years, my mom lost her marriage, her only sibling, and both her parents. Her younger sister, Judy, died of diabetic complications. Shortly after Judy's death, the phone rang early one morning at our house. A neighbor from Louisiana was calling. My mom's mother had suffered from clinical depression for much of her life—an artist, eccentric in her own ways and plagued by a disease that would not let her go. In the end, she took her own life.

In the midst of these incredible losses, my mom's beloved father developed cancer and died quickly. She loved him fiercely, and I often wonder if his death was the hardest for her to endure.

With her entire immediate family gone, the home my mom

grew up in was empty. She flew to Shreveport alone to attend to all the belongings. Like an avalanche, the world had come crashing down all at once, slipping and tumbling, burying her alive. She was lost in the landslide.

As I get older and consider what it would have been like to face what she faced in that time—and to then face the rest of her life with what was left—I often wonder how she made it. I wonder if she felt like she had lost her place in the world, as though what tied her to the earth had come undone.

She packed up my grandparents' house and loaded a moving truck with all the things she couldn't part with or couldn't sort through alone—a piano her grandmother had given her, a secretary from the living room, her mother's sewing basket, her father's toolbox, an assortment of china and silver.

Upon arriving in San Diego, my mom unloaded these heirlooms. A few things came into the house, but most went into the garage. They have sat there ever since, pushed to the corners and recesses by the overflow of our household.

My mother doesn't tend to part with things easily. She's not of the "just go buy a new one" ilk. Heritage and therefore pride reside in "the things that have been in the family for years." And every item—whether small or large—is an antique waiting to happen, an heirloom in the making. In other words, if we hold on to certain items long enough, and pass them down through enough generations, they will gain value because of their history. Even if that history is simply sitting in a box in the garage.

This is exactly the sort of mentality we were trying to address when she decided the time had come to clean out the garage. My mom accurately felt as though things had finally reached a point of insane accumulation, and she asked if I would help her do a huge cleanse. This was to be likened to the kind of cleanse

found art

someone might do to their drains or their colon or their fireplace flue. Cleaning out is really about taking inventory and making tough decisions about what needs to stay and what needs to go. Most all of our garages and lives could benefit from making a little room for the new by purging some of the old.

I took my seat on a low, white wooden stool, and Mom sat on the plastic shower seat she used when she broke her ankle in 1998 and then her foot a few years later. My friend Jamie joined us for the fun because I needed backup and someone to run to Christy's Donuts and Rubio's for sustenance.

We talked through each and every item in each and every box, making painstaking decisions associated with saying good-bye. Letting go is difficult, but the reality is, we have to let go of some things—for example, an entrenching tool from my dad's stint in ROTC (forty years ago), plastic aqua socks from a water aerobics phase (at least four pairs); tax returns from the eighties (and seventies and *sixties*). These items, though useful in their heyday, were no longer the kind of thing that needed to be "saved for someone later on." After all, "who knows when we might need them" is not a good sorting strategy. If we were going to cleanse, we needed to get tough.

Over twenty years had passed since some of the acute seasons of loss, and life was beginning to become more about the future and less about the past. So we were ready to open up the boxes and let some of today's light into yesterday's memories.

We positioned ourselves on one side of the garage, perched on our respective seats, and began. My first find was the extra-long flatbed wagon my grandfather had made for us when I was little, and immediately I could hear screams of delight echoing from the cul-de-sac at the end of the driveway.

In the elementary school years, Trey and I would steal ropes from our family tent and tie down cat-pee-stained camping mattresses to that flatbed wagon. We'd cinch and knot until we'd created a secure padding, and then we'd pile on, facedown, with the musty smell of garage and feline urine saturating the experience. We'd get our gangly neighbor, Alex (whose family, incidentally, had over twenty animals at their home), to come and join us, and all three of us would mount up with our arms and legs spread for balance.

One of the Duncan boys who lived across the street then—and still does—would whip us in circles around the cul-de-sac until all of us had been bucked off the ride. Nothing more than a poor man's wakeboarding.

With the smell of those mattresses fresh in my mind, I wheeled the wagon to the "keep" pile and began opening the boxes that had been stored just behind it. One look at the contents of the first box—my grandmother's underclothes—and I was transported.

As a child, these boxes were the magic wardrobe through which I entered other worlds. Laura and I would spend hours playing dress-up, often inviting our next-door neighbor, Allie, to join us. Laura and I were "athletic," let's say, even at twelve and seven, respectively. Allie was very tan and very skinny—birdlike, really—and she had long fingernails and went to public school. She looked a little too good in the silky satin nighties, if you know what I mean.

I loved my grandmother's old slips, especially her long, black half-slip with an elastic waist and lace trim. At least a couple times a week, I'd put that slip on my head and wear it around the house, imagining I had waist-length black hair. Sometimes I'd tie a ribbon in it or pretend to brush it with a real brush, acting foreign and exotic.

There were times, after the dress-up was over, I'd sneak back into the house with the slip still on my head and slink into the hall bathroom. I'd lock the door behind me and pull out products from beneath the bathroom sink. Secured inside, the bathroom became my stage and the mirror my audience. Many a compelling commercial was delivered in that bathroom. I sold disposable razors and shampoo, bars of soap and air freshener, gesturing dramatically like the leggy women in the nude hose and bathing suits on *The Price Is Right*.

Often, the three of us would raid the kitchen and stuff the boobs in grandmother's full slips with oranges or apples or any other round produce we could find. My mom still has pictures of Laura, Allie, and me in the front yard, striking sexy poses, with bright Valencias poking out the tops of the silky slips we had on over our clothes.

I selected a few pieces we could salvage for another generation of dress-up and handed the rest — the ones that were decomposing in my hands — to my mom to throw away.

In the next box, I dug out a holster with cap guns and a sheriff's badge. And I remembered that all I ever wanted Trey to be in our games of dress-up was "Baby Tommy," who would crawl around on the floor and want me to rock him. Once in a while, I'd also ask him to be the pet dog for us big-bosomed ladies to drag around on a leash. I didn't think either of those roles was too much to ask.

When I saw the Western ware, however, I was reminded of Trey's insistence on a different direction. No dog or baby games for him. He was Boss Hog with a cinnamon-stick cigar and a sidekick named Rosco. Occasionally I consented to play *his* game — sidling around the house with tobacco products and firearms and a Southern lilt—just as long as Rosco could have long black hair.

Partway through our sorting, we happened upon a real prize. Moms have a way of saving the strangest things related to their children. The three small plastic pillboxes we found were people's exhibit A. Each of these boxes had a name on top—Laura, Leeana, Trey. I shook mine gently, and it sounded like tiny dice in a Yahtzee cup. I gingerly opened the lid to find every single one of my baby teeth, some with roots still intact.

Upon this discovery, Jamie gave me a look from across the garage that said, *You better keep your eye on her.* I later found out that Jamie was reading a thriller about a woman who was losing her mind and using human teeth to build a floor in a dollhouse.

Every box contained a moment of my mom's life. Stacks of notebooks filled with handwritten homework assignments from college Latin courses. A small pottery vase Aunt Judy had painted and fired in an adult learning class. The first Christmas card my parents sent out as a married couple—including a black-and-white picture of them standing proudly on the grass of what is now Point Loma Nazarene University, the Pacific Ocean behind them and unforeseeable heartache ahead.

I tried my best to think of my mom as a twentysomething, which is a difficult thing to do. Often we forget our parents are real people with a real past and real pain. I tried to think about how she might have felt about herself and her life and what she wanted for her future.

Sitting in the garage—helping my mom sort through each season of her life—college, marriage, graduate school, babies, teaching, divorce, family deaths, sending kids off to college, becoming a grandmother—the size and speed of life overwhelmed me. How could a garage full of boxes capture a lifetime?

After we'd filled the trash cans a few times over, after we'd dropped off a couple carloads at Goodwill, and after we'd hosted one of our early morning garage sales, we stopped the purging and stepped back to see what kind of light had been let into the newly found corners.

With the majority of our cleaning out done, we went to dinner together. After dinner, I dropped her off at her house, and before she got out of the car, we sat in the dark driveway, staring at the closed garage door, reliving some of the past few weeks of work.

As if trying to explain things to me or to herself, my mom said, "There were times when we had so little money, Leeana. I just saved everything. I didn't know what we'd need and where it would come from. So I just kept it all. And I kept adding to it in case everything turned upside down."

In her seasons of great loss, there was no time for her to sort or process, no one to say, "Let it go." Perhaps that wouldn't have been possible anyway. She'd already had to say good-bye to so much. She needed to know she still had something to hold on to, so her garage became her savings account. As long as the boxes were full, she still had something.

Twenty-three years later, time had rolled on, the pain had dulled a bit, and she was ready to part with many things in her past.

In the dark car, we sat together in silence until my mom spoke again. "There are some things that happen in life that are difficult. And, as if you were setting a boat out to sea, you have to take those things and let them go, let them float out and away. And only God can help us do that."

letting go

Back in Bahrain, I decided I couldn't let go. I couldn't let go of my parents' divorce, of my frustrations with Steve, of the injustice of the war, of my own personal failings, of anything at all really. My mom was right, as she often is. I felt totally incapable of opening my grubby little hands on my own. Clearly, I had to let God into the whole mess.

Somehow, if we will let him, he will be the invisible glue that seeps in and re-adheres what has been ripped open. He will be the light shining into the contents of our most hidden boxes. He will soften our hearts when we can't do it on our own. He will help us turn toward each other when all we want to do is walk away. He will help us let go of our grievances when we desperately want to protect and nurture them. He will give us moments and places that will bind us together forever. All we have to do is remain the slightest bit open to becoming well.

a swatch of black silk
from a borrowed *abaya*

searching

We spun our first Christmas out of love and desert sand. Earlier in December, we had returned home to the States for Trey's wedding in Florida and a quick trip to Lake Tahoe with Steve's family. Steve needed to get back to work, so we celebrated our first Christmas at Starview.

Before we left for the States, I threw a huge party to celebrate Steve's thirtieth birthday (incidentally, both of our birthdays are in December—Steve's on the twelfth and mine on the sixteenth. When we were dating and I realized the proximity of our birthdays, I said, "Isn't it sweet that our birthdays are just four days apart," to which Steve replied in the Steve way, "Well, they have to be some time"). In addition to the *shish taook, shish kebab, toubuli, hummus,* and loads of *naan* I ordered from Al Abraaj, I wanted the flat to look festive and holiday-ready for Steve's party, so I did my best to spruce it up with what was on hand.

We had discussed getting a tree, but the very few that had been delivered to the Ship Store on base were gone in a hot second—reminiscent of Cabbage Patch Kids in the eighties. I took a chance on Mega Mart, which came through in a pinch. I purchased plastic Christmas balls in rich jewel tones that were actually great if you didn't look too closely, along with a couple of strands of icicle lights and a half dozen short red glasses to be used as votives. Ribbon was impossibly expensive, so I had to forgo further embellishments, but the Christmas balls and candlelight were enough to make a statement.

The footed trifle dish Mr. Sharif had left for us was lovely. Filled with the Mega Mart balls, it worked perfectly as a centerpiece on our dining room table. I draped the coffee table with icicle lights and lined up the red votives on the entry table with a large glass flower vase in the middle that was full of more balls. Little angels my mom had sent me heralded the holidays in certain strategic locations around the flat. Somehow the whole hodgepodge worked—unconventional yet celebratory.

I couldn't help but laugh when we gave directions to Starview for Steve's big party. You couldn't decipher a left-brained way to tell people how to get to our place. Because of the whole no-paved-road thing, we had to guide people using landmarks, especially at night. No problem. As soon as the sun went down, the timer was tripped, and the huge Starview star began to razzle and dazzle against the darkening sky like a pyrotechnic light show. The star looked like something off the Vegas Strip, oversized and gaudy and generally out of place in its surroundings but particularly helpful in giving directions. *Come down the street by the Grand Mosque toward the base. Our building is on the left alongside a handful of other high-rises. There's no sign or paved road, so look for the building with the giant star on top, and just follow the star.*

They did just that, and we toasted Steve's life with friends we had not known even a few months before. The boys puffed *Romeo y Julietas* by the windows, while the girls sat in circles, eating *hummus* and gossiping as only military wives can do.

Following the star is an ancient tradition dating back to that first Christmas when the angel told the Magi to journey through the Middle Eastern desert to find the Christ child. They climbed aboard their camels and began searching for this Promised One. *We observed a star in the eastern sky that signaled his birth*, the ancient astrologers said. *We're on a pilgrimage to worship him*. Their journey of holy significance ended at the feet of the newborn King.

In those days, not dissimilar to these days, the world was waiting for a savior. Israel was expecting deliverance and the promised messiah — high-profile royalty — who would come to save them. The last place anyone expected to find this long-awaited king was in a barn in Bethlehem. Certainly no one was expecting a baby from the body of a virgin teen. But as we know, that is exactly how Jesus came.

The moment he entered our world, all of humanity breathed again, as the way out of the darkness — the way out of our eternal lostness — had been found. The light of life lived, though our freedom would cost him his life. I wonder if anyone who came to see the holy infant remembered what had been foretold: that he would one day be pierced for our transgressions, crushed for our iniquities, his life a guilt offering, his death-wounds our healing, and his resurrection our hope. In the sheer bliss of new-born life, I doubt anyone considered the great price that would be paid on the cross for our living-lost souls.

Few things are more terrifying than being lost. I was really scared only a handful of times in Bahrain. Once when the overly zealous Pakistani construction crew began drilling a foundation for a high-rise of flats so close to our building that it made all of Starview sway and shake like we lived on a fault line. Once when I was absolutely sure someone had put an explosive device under my car while I was out shopping. (Turns out I was just paranoid.) Once when Steve had to take a trip to Iraq for a week, and I couldn't tell a single soul. Once when I almost got shot coming on base because I was talking on my cell phone and not paying attention. And once when Steve and I were taking advantage of a rare-day-off Saturday and got lost. We happened on to black Sabbath in Shi'a town when we were just searching for a furniture store.

I'm actually surprised we only managed to find ourselves really turned around on that one fateful day. Bahrain is famous for unmarked streets and roundabouts that gnarl together to create a confusing mess of options. Ridiculously itty-bitty street signs are posted here and there, but — wouldn't you know it — they're in Arabic, which isn't particularly helpful if you don't speak the language.

When Steve and I turned the corner and inadvertently entered the hopelessly small one-way Shi'a street, we knew immediately we were stuck. We couldn't go backward, and we could barely crawl forward, the crowd closing in on us from every side. Somehow, and this was growing clearer by the minute, we had taken a wrong turn and happened upon what seemed to be a farmers market at the gates of hell.

Everything was black. Every person, every storefront, every sign, every surface was swathed in or painted black. Dark, massive banners splattered with Arabic graffiti stretched across the roads and above every sidewalk. Hulking black tents were erected on the sides of the road, further narrowing the treacherous alleyways. Hordes of people thronged the streets, chanting in response to angry men yelling into microphones set up on each corner. Men with long black whips cracked the tails across their own shoulders and backs and wailed with each strike. Black flags billowed and flapped in the air like angry crows. Huge portraits of sad-looking, liquid-eyed Muslim men peppered the walls of every building, each one of them staring right at us.

Inch by inch, Steve nudged our car down a street no wider than a queen-size mattress. Shi'a men stooped over and peered into the windows of our car. Stupid Americans. I slid deeper into my seat, trying to avoid their eyes.

As angry men-in-black shouted around us, I began imagining how they might pull us from our car onto the sweltering sidewalks of Shi'a town, where we would be strung up before the frothing crowds. I prayed the most sacred breath prayer I could think to pray, "Holy crap, holy crap, holy crap," begging God for amnesty with every fretful pant. Steve sat in stressed silence, with eyes piercing through the windshield.

I broke in with my typically helpful passive-aggressiveness, "Uh, babe? Do you think this is where we want to be? I'm wondering if we took a wrong turn." To which Steve was probably thinking, "Wrong turn? I hadn't even noticed."

After a few tense minutes, Steve turned a corner, and we were miraculously delivered onto a much wider, much less crowded road leading away from the demonstration. Later, we found out we had driven right into a holiday celebration commemorating some of the earliest Shi'a martyrs.

I imagine that must have been a little like how it felt in the years leading up to the first Christmas — the world stuck in Shi'a town with all of its scary blackness and whips and graffiti, searching for some kind of savior. In one magical moment of miraculous deliverance, the light had come. The dawn had broken. No one ever had to live lost again. There, in the form of a precious babe, was God with us.

Our first Christmas was strange and unlike any we've had since, but perhaps that's the true spirit of Christmas. Displaced travelers in a foreign land, far away from family, making do with what's on hand—all with a star shining overhead.

Like the Magi, I observed the star in the eastern sky, and I, too—in my own way and in my own space and in my own time—was on a pilgrimage to worship the Christ child.

15

embracing

The Middle East has an ancient wedding tradition I experienced in Bahrain. The bride's family buys the most expensive incense they can afford and ceremoniously invites her to stand over the incense to be perfumed the day of her wedding. The aromatic scent saturates her undergarments, her wedding dress, her body, and her hair, perfuming her from head to toe with a lasting and expensive scent.

My taking part in this tradition had nothing to do with a wedding at all, actually. It all started when a Navy wife invited me to brunch. I wasn't particularly interested in going to brunch with strangers until she mentioned we would be dining at a Bahraini woman's home. At the mention of this detail, I perked up and agreed to go.

We survived the jostling stretch of unpaved dirt we had to cross to get from the main paved road to Nawal's villa. My car perched on a dangerously acute angle, and as we tumbled out of my car, I felt like Noah exiting the ark atop Mount Ararat. We had been asked to dress conservatively out of respect for Nawal and her home, so I wore an ankle-length linen dress with a long-sleeved linen shirt as a sort of jacket. The morning was far too warm to have so many clothes on, and the polyester lining of my dress stuck to the back of my legs like hair gel.

Nawal was not what I expected. She was neither serious nor aloof, or even all that mysterious. In fact, she seemed like someone who could probably throw a good party. Unexpectedly plump and jovial, she hugged me a little too tight when we stepped inside the entryway of her home.

Her husband was quite the opposite—a Jack Sprat of a man—thin and nervous and clearly unprepared for the descending of so many unfamiliar women. We were welcomed graciously and shown into the parlor, where I gave Nawal a hostess gift of American chocolates. She proudly presented me with a tapestry bag containing printed fabrics to be used for head coverings. After gifts, we were escorted to the living room for our meal.

Platters of eggs, rice, fish paste, fresh naan, and ancient-looking teapots of strong Middle Eastern tea covered the large cloth spread out on the living room floor where we were instructed to sit. Nawal's husband hid from our group after brief introductions, and her preteen daughter shuttled food back and forth from the kitchen to the meal at Nawal's command.

A dozen of us sat around the "table"—friends of Nawal's, friends of friends of Nawal's, and a couple other strays like me. I didn't know a single person at the brunch except the Navy wife I'd come with—and she and I knew little more about each other than names. We all lounged together, talking and eating, the international language fluently spoken by women worldwide. We were a mishmash of *abayas*, housecoats, and ankle-length dresses.

After the meal, Nawal produced an incense stand and invited me into the middle of the room, maybe in the way we might pull out a game of Twister. She placed a pungent-smelling musk incense on the stand and lit the bottom until smoke billowed out from the incense. She asked me to put one foot on either side.

With the rest of the room watching, foreign faces smiling up at me from their seats on the floor, I placed my feet about shoulder width apart on either side of the incense stand while Nawal bloused the skirt of my dress around the now-flowing smoke.

The scented smoke floated up my skirt, into my dress, out the top of my shirt, up through my hair, wafting ever so effortlessly toward the ceiling. I couldn't feel it so much as just sense it surrounding me, saturating my clothes and skin and hair with heavy musk. I remember feeling typically self-conscious on the surface — uncomfortable from the staring strangers — but something deep down inside me felt different. The deeper, truer me was lifted right out of that living room.

The summer after my sophomore year I worked at a camp in the Ozark Mountains. I and another twenty-year-old counseled a cabin of ten sixteen-year-old girls, which turned out to be truly the adventure you might assume when you even imagine ten sixteen-year-old girls together in one place.

Camp had its way with us all, as it had been designed to do — reducing us to best friends in about a week and encouraging us to do what we would have never done outside its confines. In addition to the twenty or so days we spent in camp, we also spent five days out in the wilderness together, braving team-bonding games, rappelling towering rocks, suffering sunburned scalps from long days of canoeing, and teetering across treetop ropes courses. We learned how to pee in the woods and take showers in the river. We were even forced to endure hanging out with the hot wilderness guides who had to take their shirts off due to the unrelenting heat of Missouri at that time of the year. Somehow we managed.

Until right now, I never really considered the enormity of the situation. Ten sets of parents thought it reasonable for me, a twenty-year-old city girl, to take their precious daughters into the wilderness for five days with only the help of another clueless twenty-year-old and some shirtless guys. In the moment, the responsibility didn't feel so weighty. As far as I was concerned, we were in it together. I was as wide-eyed as those girls and every bit as eager. We were an unlikely tribe, a Band of Sisters, marching through the back country with the sweet smell of youth on us. It was a wild and lucky summer. And something whispered that to me from my first days there.

All counselors were required to arrive a few weeks early and help prepare the grounds for the campers. After long days of working—raking leaves, cleaning bathrooms, planning activities—we'd congregate in each other's cabins. One night, a plan developed for a late-night walk.

Suddenly, we were hushing each other as we snuck outside, falling into a single-file line on our way out the door. One of the last girls in our string of eight grabbed her guitar from the corner—which I considered aggressively overspiritual—and we were off into the night.

Night is an understatement. The world was black. Ozark dark. Two steps out the door, and our giggling immediately stopped, each groping for the girl directly in front of her. We inched forward as our eyes adjusted ever so slightly, and in a matter of minutes we were swallowed by the mountain.

The leaves and branches crunched under our feet—the only noise you could hear. Until the girl with the guitar at the end of the line started playing, spontaneously. In one moment this was predictable and annoying, but in the next, I gave in to the anonymity of the darkness and the other mysteries in our midst. We began to sing into the night, an impromptu choir.

We sang—loudly—serenading the trees and stars and cabins along our path. I'm sure we sang other songs, but I only remember singing one over and over. It's a song I still sing from time to time at church, and it never ceases to take me back to the darkness of that humid camp night when we were high up, within an arm's reach of heaven.

As our voices echoed in the mountain air, I found myself quieted and present, a sense of reverence replacing my initial uneasiness. I was aware of something in our midst.

Everyone expects to be close to God at camp, to cry and make promises and leave repentant and resolved. I assumed that would happen during the last week at the last bonfire when the camp speaker was goading the masses toward some predetermined action or decision. But my assumptions got the better of me in the end.

God was there. We did nothing to conjure his presence. He just came near. And somehow, in the black night of the Ozarks, we could see him. Like the cloud of incensed smoke billowing around me in Nawal's living room, I couldn't so much feel him as just sense him, surrounding and saturating me on that strange night.

The day after we went to Nawal's, I woke up with the scent of musk in my room. My linen dress would have to be dry-cleaned in order to get the aroma out, and my hair and skin would have to be scrubbed. That's God, right, the strong presence in and through everything that we can neither see nor touch.

I often wonder where God is, what he's up to, how he's

moving, when his plan will unfold. I wrestle with all sorts of puzzling God questions, and though I try not to get too frustrated or confused, I'm not great at two of the main ingredients required in living by faith: (1) waiting and (2) staying calm. I just want God to tell me what to do. Maybe more than anything, I want him to tell me everything is going to be OK, that he's with me, and that something good is around the corner. So often, though, he seems out of reach, his voice is hard to hear, and his plan feels foggy.

Though painstakingly difficult, I try my very best to hold on to Jesus' words in the Beatitudes: *You're blessed when you feel you've lost what is most dear to you* (answers and assurances are certainly most dear to me). *Only then can you be embraced by the one most dear to you.* I try to trust that these words are true and that they are for me today. I try to believe what I know to be true, that God is often waiting for us in the least-expected, least-desired places — fear, grief, loneliness, confusion, forgiveness, shame, the Ozarks, Nawal's villa.

After all, if he can show up in a burning bush, or all of a sudden in an upper room, or in a garden three days after he had died, or in a pillar of fire in the sky, then why can't he show up in some similarly strange and wonderful places?

Perhaps if God were able to find me way up on a mountaintop in the Ozarks and wrap himself around me in the black night air, and if he were able to find me in the living room of a Bahraini villa — ten thousand miles away from familiar — and wrap himself around me in the musky smoke of wedding incense, then just maybe he might also be able to find me in the midst of my in-need faith and wrap himself around me with his God-embrace. In time, I might even be able to embrace him back.

16
dying

Less than one mile from the base — and therefore Steve — and less than half a mile from the Grand Mosque — and therefore God — Starview sat right between two of the most important landmarks in my Bahraini life.

Let me explain.

Like Protestant churches in the Bible Belt, hundreds of mosques bespeckle Bahrain. Some resemble opulent shrines or museums, created more to look at than to use. Others are more like village outposts where all the locals congregate. In addition to all these less-grand mosques, there is the singular *Grand* Mosque. Every Muslim country has one — the official Islam headquarters where visitors are welcomed and shown around, where a huge library is housed, and where education is conducted in addition to the Friday services.

I've been inside the huge teak double doors twice — once with another Navy wife the first week we moved to Bahrain and once when my mother-in-law came to visit us a few months later. The first time I went to the mosque, I met Fatima, a young mosque volunteer who showed us around in a guided tour of sorts. The second time I went, I requested Fatima as our guide.

In fact, I went back with my mother-in-law for the sole purpose of seeing her again.

Like the meat market, the Grand Mosque intrigues me. I am drawn to the tall minarets like I am the skinned lamb flung across the man's shoulders.

A receptionist greets us when we enter the huge front doors and escorts us to the library where we are asked to wait for Fatima. While we wait, the same receptionist instructs us to leave our shoes in the cubbies in the entryway right outside the library and hands us an *abaya* and an oversized head scarf, both of which we are asked to put on.

I have never worn an *abaya* before. The closest I've ever come is the polyester gown I wore when I graduated from college. The *abaya* is far more filmy and flimsy, and it floats right over my head and all the way down to the ground like a giant black parachute. Though the smell of someone else's deodorant is caught in the fibers, I don't really care. I feel a bit scandalous and free, which are two of the best feelings in the world.

I was raised to be a Christian. Every aspect of my upbringing was based on the assumption that I would embrace Christ at a young age and follow him to an old age. This speaks to the unwavering faith and conviction of my parents. They raised me to be a person congruent with their beliefs, which is how parents should raise children, if you ask me.

As expected, I accepted Christ and the message of Christianity as a young child. I was a Christian in the way that I was a girl, an American, a daughter, a blonde—I fell into it through DNA and good fortune. In fact, I don't remember being anything other than a Christian in the same way that I don't remember being anything other than a girl, an American, a daughter, and a blonde.

found art

Throughout my entire life, I have spoken Christian, dressed Christian, studied Christian, dated Christian, sang Christian, read Christian, and usually thought Christian. I have simply been immersed in Christianity in the very same way that Fatima had been immersed in Islam.

A possible consequence of this immersion was that my faith had become rehearsed and ingrained and flat. I believe God knew all this — that I was lulled and tired. He felt forever away, and I felt an all-pervasive numbness, though I knew what to say and think to convince myself otherwise.

I arrived at the mosque with all this in tow. As I slipped into the *abaya*, I felt like I was doing something brave and totally different from anything I had ever done. I felt like I was walking headlong into that meat market I had once been so scared to set foot in.

Fatima appears. She is tiny, a baby bird in all black. She cannot be over five-foot-one or -two and must weigh right around a hundred pounds. Her body is a child's. Nipped in at the waist, her *abaya* hints at a woman's figure with the illusion of a waist and hips, though she has no curves to fill it out. Excess fabric pools on the floor at her feet and trails behind her like a long black train when she walks. I find myself looking at her for what are probably awkward amounts of time. She introduces herself and tells us she is nineteen years old, a university student, and a volunteer tour guide at the mosque.

"Follow me," she says.

As we begin walking into the main prayer hall, I notice silky black socks occasionally peeking out from the generous hemline of Fatima's *abaya*. No feet showing. As she gestures toward the women's prayer balcony, her sleeve slips up to reveal the fingertips of black gloves. No hands showing.

Actually, her eyes are the only feature I can really see on her entire body. But the eyes, as they say, are the window to the soul. Certainly true in this case. Black-brown and round, they give off warmth and depth. Her head is covered with a long black piece of silk fabric many of the women wear in town. It covers her hair, forehead, the sides of her face, and her nose and below—including her mouth, chin, and neck. Nothing showing but the eyes.

Talking casually with someone who is completely covered is a strange phenomenon. I have seen women who are similarly covered conversing with each other, but I've never actually talked with a woman, for any length of time, who was wearing this kind of veil. I find myself looking past the visible trying to imagine the invisible. As she talks, I try to picture the shape of her face hidden under all the layers of fabric. Thin and small like the rest of her? Or round and youthful like her eyes?

"Do you ever take off your veil?" I ask.

"At home when I am not in the room with my brothers or their friends," she says.

I totally get it, I overeagerly thought to myself. *When I was in high school, my mom wouldn't let me wear a two-piece swimsuit in the pool if my little brother's friends were over.* Not exactly apples to apples.

It didn't occur to me at the time, but I later wondered if her father required her to be completely covered in order to work at the mosque. He probably knew she would be coming into contact with non-Muslims, including men, and I bet he wanted to protect her from exposing anything other than what was absolutely necessary.

Fatima continues our tour, pointing out even the smallest details and features of the mosque.

Twenty-three-foot doors made from solid Indian teak frame the entrance with solemnity. Nine hundred fifty-two handblown French lamps, each a gorgeous glass globe, hang overhead like floating bubbles throughout every inch of the mosque. The world's largest fiberglass dome, visible from the exterior, spans the entire ceiling of the main prayer hall. Yard after endless yard of custom Scottish carpet lines any space not covered by the nearly ten thousand square feet of Italian marble in the prayer halls and the courtyard. The *pièce de résistance* is the three-ton Austrian crystal chandelier that hangs from the dome in the center of the main prayer hall. The constant mix of natural light from the inner courtyard and incandescent light cast by the globes and chandelier creates a glow that is both extravagant and pure. The effect is paradise.

At capacity, the mosque accommodates seven thousand worshipers throughout the main prayer hall, the balcony, the women's prayer hall, and the courtyard, spreading the crowd over tens of thousands of square feet. The acoustics are uniquely designed to allow the Imam to stand in the middle of the main prayer hall, under the fiberglass dome, and every worshiper in the entire mosque can hear him perfectly without a single microphone or speaker.

Every detail has a story, every story a tradition, and every tradition a significance. Standing in my floor-length borrowed black *abaya*, surrounded by European glass and spiritual devotion, I'm absorbed. I am caught off guard when Fatima turns and looks at me, there in the main prayer hall, and I notice tears in her eyes. Glistening from the glow of the lighted bubbles floating all around us, her eyes lock on to mine, and I stand very still.

"Many people think we do these prayers out of duty or fear,

but it is not so," she says. "They are my offering. They are my worship. I do them because I love God."

When Fatima spoke—for the first time in a long time—I really listened to what was being said about God. Between the lines was an entire sermon on faith. I really listened to that too. In my lifetime, I have probably heard thousands of messages on believing, but no message has ever reached inside me like hers did. I really heard her, and by proxy, I believe I heard him.

Seeing Fatima's teary eyes and authentic confession made me want what she had. Not Islam or Allah or the *abaya*, but a sense of devotion and passion that made faith seem like a choice and a practice and a pursuit and not merely a hole in the ground I had fallen into and was now stuck in.

In some ways, this was my first moment of believing in all my life. Technically—on the books—I had been believing for about twenty-five years prior, but something very true shifted in my heart that felt like an old thing had died and a new thing arrived to take its place. I think what arrived was *desire*, if I were to put a word to it.

I saw fire in Fatima—active and engaged—and it flew in the face of my passive, fallen-into faith. When I watched Fatima, I realized I had given up on the inside. My outsides were still pleasantries and platitudes, but my insides were paralyzed. I confronted in that moment how much I loathed this disparate, fraudulent thing that I was so deftly living. I realized I envied her. I was that stupid fly, yet again, bulldozing my brains into the same old walls of trying and failing. She had found the open door.

Fatima should have been repressed and glazed. She is the one forced to cover herself from head to toe, forced to pray in a separate room from the men at her place of worship, forced to live in almost complete anonymity from the rest of the world. She should be angry, I believe. She should feel cheated by these rules and restrictions. Yet, she seemed deeply devoted and at the same time deeply free.

That beautiful mosque, with the sun-soaked inner courtyard, made me want to believe again, or maybe for the first time. I wanted to go home and be quiet—not "have a quiet time," but just be quiet and sit in my desire to know God and to hear him and to love him. I think that means I wanted to pray, which I had no memory of ever *wanting* to do before.

Maybe I should have been thinking about all the reasons Fatima was misguided. Maybe I should have even been trying to talk with her about these things. But I didn't want to. Instead, I wanted to hear her. I wanted to care about my faith the way she cared about hers. I wanted to love Jesus, no matter what it cost me. I wanted to cry because I was so moved by how his death has given me life. I wanted to pore over the Bible the way she pored over the Qur'an.

The layers of numbness began dying a slow death that day. In their place sparked an inkling of desire. And desire, as we all know, is the most scandalous freedom there is.

17

scattering

The desire that ignited in the Grand Mosque continued to burn low and hot inside me. For the first time since I could remember, a true spiritual longing settled in. I didn't know what to do with it at first, and I was worried I would scare off this little piece of my soul like you might scare off a skittish fawn. I knew things could go either way — this would become a turning point in my spiritual life, or it would turn out like all the other short-lived attempts I'd made to connect with God.

I had faced disappointment before — many times. In the past, I had felt shifts inside myself and believed that something big enough had happened that I could sustain the energy and momentum. After a short stint of trying and striving and doing all the things I knew to do, I would start to feel the numbness creeping back in. I would give in to it every time because I didn't know what else to do. This has been my spiritual pattern — exhausting and disenchanting.

Sometimes my disappointment locks on to the church and I want to blame my spiritual dissatisfaction on the messages and mantras I have heard so many times. Convincing myself that the church has let me down is convenient and pain free. I don't have to take any responsibility. Sometimes my disappointment is with God and how he seems so close to everyone else but never close enough to me. Though I want to believe he is the one to blame, convincing myself that God is at fault is a little more difficult because, after all, he is God. Probably most often, my disappointment is really with myself. If I were better—if I were one of the good people—I would feel as though I were walking hand in hand with God during every moment of every day. Because I don't feel such true intimacy much of the time, I am flawed.

This mind-set of flawedness keeps me at arm's length from God, I'm convinced. I sabotage myself spiritually. *No matter what I do, I will end up failing,* I tell myself. *I will never be able to do enough for God to really love me.* I give up before I've even begun.

I am badly abused when it comes to believing. I have suffered the abuse at my own hands. I have absolutely done a number on myself after all these years of being a Christian. I have fed myself some pretty awful lies and believed them, and I have tied all of that wrong thinking into God. Numbness has felt like the safest option. Going through the motions, putting on a happy face, talking the talk—whatever you want to call it—I've been doing this disingenuous dance with myself. Right under the numbness is a corrosive fatigue.

Since the Grand Mosque, I started sitting on the floor in Starview once a day. I was leery about categorizing this practice as a spiritual discipline for fear that I would then not want to do it. I found it much easier to rhetorically trick myself by simply saying I was "sitting on the floor." Harmless.

In doing this, I realized how spiritually neurotic and slightly conspiratorial I've been allowing myself to be. I decided to start with what I could do that felt true and real, with what I wanted to do, not what I thought I needed to do in order to gain a sort of approval or worthiness.

In the spirit of authenticity, I managed to sit on the floor without getting agitated and anxious. I was also able to close my eyes a little and even write a few things in a notebook (though this was by no means "prayer" or "journaling").

That was about as much as I could do because anything more felt like pressure, specifically pressure to produce (which is one of the drugs I was just then starting to detox from). Before you know it, I'd be trying to perform, and that wary little four-legged creature that was just starting to poke its head out of the woods would be off and running.

I didn't make a mental note of what I hoped to produce from the time on the floor or set a "goal," per se. I wasn't trying to "get anything out of it" in the Christiany way people might ask, "So, what are you getting out of your quiet time these days?" I didn't actually expect that I would get anything done. I wasn't "working through" anything as you might say you are "working through the book of Proverbs" or you are "working through the Pauline Epistles." I was just sitting, and, well, maybe closing my eyes here and there for brief stints.

I tried to do things I might enjoy, such as propping myself up on oversized Middle Eastern floor cushions (because, again, the floor feels organic and unofficial), lighting a candle or two (because I love candles), turning on a soulful song with lots of violins (because, honestly, it makes me feel fondly melancholy), and closing my eyes (again, briefly, and only when I wanted to).

I am well aware of how temperamental I sound, like a poodle who needs his food cut up a certain way or like Howard Hughes. Oh, well. Sometimes we have to start over, and that is what I was doing. I was learning to create a safe space for my

found art

soul to come out of hiding, and I have never done that before in my life.

In addition, I was trying to breathe on this tiny little ember of desire that had sparked in the mosque with Fatima. I didn't want to blow too hard for fear of extinguishing it, so I had to start slow, with kind and easy breaths.

One other really big thing helped.

I remember the first time I heard the call to prayer in Starview. Of course, I had heard the customary Muslim chant before. Every day, five times a day, the sound carried all over Juffair and even made its way past the barbed wire-topped cement walls and the barricaded entrances of the base so that if you were sitting at the pool or playing volleyball on the sand courts or sitting on top of a picnic bench cleaning your gun (which the Marines did daily), you would hear the call.

The first time the words rang through Starview was different though. I'm not sure why—other than the fact that I had been to the mosque by then and perhaps my ears were hearing things in a new way, as is the case when an awakening happens.

I was standing in the kitchen, mid-morning, washing dishes and looking out onto the little patch of Gulf I could see from the window above the kitchen sink. The *muezzin* began, *Aaallaaahu Akbar! Aaallaaahu Akbar!* God is greatest! God is greatest! The sound was emphatic and earnest, with long, drawn-out syllables.

The Shamal picked up each and every sound and delivered every last inflection to my doorstep, and what I heard was so loud and so intense that I could have sworn the entire world was in earshot. The cadence was slow with a sincere longing—much how I felt inside. I heard in the call to prayer the same thing I saw in Fatima's eyes.

I felt weird and self-conscious, as though someone were watching me, and yet I also felt quiet and open. In the words of the call to prayer, I heard a message that went something like: *Leeana, it is not all up to you.* I don't know how I heard those words, other than I knew, like I knew in the Ozarks and at Nawal's villa and at the Grand Mosque, that God was speaking to me through an unlikely source. I knew, in the deepest part of my being, that he had come for me. He had followed the star!

With my hands still in the soapy water, and the call to prayer echoing through my eat-in kitchen, I started to cry. The small ember of desire was fanned into the tiniest flame. I finally got what was in front of me all along: it wasn't all up to me.

God had taken me by the hand so I could walk. He had replaced my heart of stone with a heart of flesh. He had given me a new name. He had called me his own. He had given me rest. He had sent his Son. He had come—in the Gulf and the call to prayer and the *souq* and Capital Centre and Starview and the meat market—he had come.

He did not forget.

He did not lose track.

He did not give up.

He found me on the far side of the sea.

The embers burned hotter still and flared up into the beginnings of a flame. The flame, though small and nascent, consumed what was left of the tepid numbness. The remains—the sticky and substantive ashes of personal striving—were scattered all throughout the sands of Bahrain. And I sat back down on the floor.

a mesquite leaf

peace

Just when I started to settle and feel a sense of balance and comfort, the whole adventure was ending. Isn't that life? Always a trick up her sleeve to keep us from feeling too oriented or calm.

We received orders back to San Diego, something we had hoped would happen, and we began thinking about what it would be like to return "home." Though I was returning to something that should have felt familiar to me, San Diego was now a world away.

I wasn't the only one facing the dread of leaving. Right before Steve's tour ended, the base was turned upside down by some very sobering events.

News came in about a terrorist attack in Saudi Arabia, and the rumor mill on base began churning. Four terrorists infiltrated a foreign workers housing compound in Khobar, Eastern Saudi, and held more than fifty residents hostage. The hostages were workers from a handful of different countries who were in Saudi to work for a high-paying, foreign oil company. After twenty-four hours had passed, Saudi Special Forces surrounded the compound in broad daylight, attempting to flush out the terrorists. One was captured, but the other three escaped in a stolen car, leaving behind dead and wounded hostages. Some speculated that the Saudi Special Forces were complicit in the attack, allowing the terrorists to escape.

Twenty-five hostages were injured, another twenty-two killed. The terrorist group claiming responsibility said they were after the "Crusaders" who were in Saudi Arabia "stealing our oil and our resources." Most of those killed had admitted to being Christians when asked, and most of those spared had claimed to be Muslim. The incident was a wholesale slaughtering that happened very, very close to Bahrain, just a little over eight miles from Starview.

A few miles and a causeway over the Gulf are all that separate Bahrain and Saudi. Khobar is on the Bahraini side, so concern was in the air. The proximity wasn't the only issue. The causeway was also problematic because unmonitored access created a porous border between the two countries. Saudis could easily come over to Bahrain, and many did so on the weekends to enjoy certain "luxuries" the *Sharia* law doesn't allow—alcohol, prostitution, driving, less covering (for the women), and the ever-popular Gulf Hotel. The military higher-ups were worried that those responsible for the massacre would be coming to Bahrain next.

We heard from a few different sources that the base admiral was considering a mandatory evacuation of all U.S. military dependents from Bahrain. If the evacuation happened, all children and spouses of active-duty military personnel would have to leave the country within just a few weeks.

The wives in our command were drowning in the thought of facing separation from their husbands. So many of those we met had planned on living in Bahrain for years. The tour provided a good life. The standard of living was better than most could afford in the States, the schools were private and very good, and most families were able to stay together instead of being separated by deployments. I felt a low-grade panic present in all our circles.

As timing would have it, we were in an entirely different situation. I tried not to make too big a deal out of this. Our tour was days away from being finished when the Khobar massacre happened. We already had our orders. The Navy had already come and packed our entire house, except for a couple of suitcases. A good number of our worldly possessions were on a boat headed to Southern California. If the evacuation were to take place, we wouldn't be directly affected.

Many of our friends, however, were facing an unknown duration of separation, and this prospect sent a few into full-blown denial. Some seemed convinced the evacuation would never happen, that the admiral wouldn't enforce such a fate after all. All forms of optimism turned out to be wishful thinking.

The rumors were soon confirmed, and dependents were ordered to evacuate Bahrain within three weeks due to threats against Westerners and credible evidence concerning plans to carry out some form of terrorism in Bahrain within the year. By the time the evacuation was officially announced, Steve and I had our plane tickets in hand.

Overnight, hundreds of families began saying good-bye. Some military personnel only had a few months left on their orders, and they'd be able to join their families relatively soon, but some had arrived days before the evacuation was announced and would spend the full two years of their tour unaccompanied.

Families began making preparations to leave immediately. Because of the short notice, no one could pack up their homes or ship their cars to their next residence. Everyone was instructed to pack a few suitcases and leave. Some of the wives at our command moved in with their parents back in the States, while some lived in hotels for months until they could find a more permanent home. Many families had sold their homes in the States before moving to Bahrain, so they had nothing to return to. I overheard one wife say through tears, "Well, I guess we'll just pick a state."

Those days marked traumatic times. Not only was the war still hot and heavy just two hundred miles away in Iraq; the relative calm of life in Bahrain was coming to an end. Liberty restrictions increased, parents pulled their kids out of schools, and families started saying good-bye. I remember walking into the gym on base where intramural basketball games were held. The courts were covered with countless rectangular folding tables. Huge lines snaked around the perimeter of the court. One area was reserved for medical records pickup. One contained all the forms for transporting pets. At another set of tables, there were forms for forwarding mail. In line, mothers hugged each other and tried to keep their sense of humor through the whole ordeal. I doubt any of them ever imagined they'd become refugees.

Though many still believed the evacuation would be temporary and dependents would be brought back in a few weeks or months, the ban was never lifted.

On our last night at Starview, I snuck away and stood at one of the floor-to-ceiling windows that lined our living room and faced the Gulf. I breathed in one more moment, one more sunset, one more look at the horizon, knowing that I might be one of the last wives to take in that particular vantage point.

I could see the men from our building—the Nepalese

found art

gatekeeper and Mohammed and another young guy who washed cars for spare change—downstairs talking and laughing about something, their shirts billowing on their backs as the wind swept by. The orange and blue dump trucks, quiet after a day of loading and hauling, sat in front of our building like toy trucks waiting to be pushed around in the dirt the next morning. Stray dogs barked and chased the occasional passing car. The sun burned in the sky as it set. To the north I could see the cupolas of the Grand Mosque in the distance, at any moment ready to commence the call to prayer. The intense orange sky played against the pale monochrome of the sand and sand-colored buildings.

I'd called for the Chinese takeout. I was waiting for Steve to get home so we could enjoy our last night together in our flat. The evening was bittersweet. I opened the window and closed my eyes as the cool air from the flat mixed with the hot breeze outside.

Shortly after, the call to prayer came rushing in, and I stood at the window listening for the last time. *Aaallaaaahu Akbar! Aaallaaaahu Akbar!*

Before we arrived in Bahrain, I had never heard the call to prayer before. The words meant nothing to me. I remember the first time I really heard them as I stood in the kitchen at Starview. I remember what it felt like to sense that God was speaking to me through those words, as if somehow he was using something unfamiliar to break through the numbness and get my attention.

It's strange how life often requires something foreign to connect us with something that, in the end, was so close all along. Sometimes we need a change of scenery in order to see what is really there inside us—all the parts and pieces of ourselves that have somehow been lost but are in desperate need of finding again.

Allahu Akbar! Allahu Akbar! the familiar sound hit my ears again. No longer was I nervously perched on the rung of performance or appearances; no longer was I dangerously imbalanced on the tightropes of managing or striving; no longer was I seductively removed from the realities of pain and healing. I was still.

As the smothering outside air continued to commingle with the cool inside air, I wondered how I was going to go about the task of holding on to the inner world as my outer world was about to change yet again. I had no idea what lay ahead — the difficulties of assimilating my new self with my old world, the struggle to keep our marriage alive, the attempts to salvage the learnings of Bahrain. I had no idea, and so I just stayed still, as I had learned to do in Capital Centre and again in that very flat. I reveled in that one moment of peace. Even as the world continued to unfold in violence and volatility, I stood quietly at the window.

I remember looking out the window at Capital Centre and staring out at the Gulf for what seemed like hours. I would pull back the heavy green drapes in the master bedroom almost every day in those first few weeks and just look out, wide-eyed, like a shy teenager at a school dance. I wanted to walk across the room and really strut my stuff, but I was desperately afraid and unsure. The night we arrived, I felt trapped inside myself, numb to the world, not sure if I had gained more or lost more by coming to a new place.

Over time, I learned I had gained *and* lost. Any season of life worth its salt, any season that really transforms us, will bring both in equal measure. I lost some tears and gained some healing. I lost some numbness and gained some desire. I lost some pain and gained some beauty. I lost some falseness and gained some freedom. I lost my bearings and gained some trust.

The war raged on, terrorists attacked, evacuations began, but I drank in the skyline of calm in that one parenthetical moment between what had been and what would be. The world was absolutely buzzing with the electric shock of chaos—as it almost always is—and I stood and looked out my window at nothing in particular and at everything.

killing

A few weeks before we moved home to the States, Steve and I left Bahrain for a short visit to Sicily. As soon as he turned over his duties to his replacement, we had a window of time to take a quick trip before we needed to be back in Bahrain for our final checkout.

We chose Sicily because of the military rotator flight that flew between the base in Bahrain and the U.S. base in Sigonella, Sicily. The flight left at 2:00 a.m., but what did we care? The round-trip fare for each ticket was $26. Done deal.

Steve and I made absolutely no plans or reservations anywhere, except with the rental car shack across the street from the flight terminal in Sigonella. Our only itinerary was to drive until we were ready to stop and to move on to the next city when we were ready to go.

We didn't tour sites or try to pick up on the language. We did what anyone who visits Italy must spend the majority of their time doing: we ate and ate and ate—pizza margherita with thin crust, gnocchi gorgonzola, crispy calamari. We drank red wine and cappuccinos every day, and we sat out in the piazzas and held hands. We bought a few pieces of hand-painted pottery at outdoor markets, and we took absolutely every possible opportunity to walk out into the Mediterranean.

The trip was simple and perfect—and the first time I realized Steve and I existed as an entity beyond Bahrain and the military and the dailyness of our lives in the Middle East. After spending a year building our marriage in Bahrain, I needed to know that "home" was wherever we were together and not just something we had created in one place. I found out that our relationship could pack up and travel nicely, like the bathing suit and gauzy wrap I had brought to Italy. This revelation came just in time, as, unbeknownst to me at that moment, I would call on its truth in coming weeks and months.

In Cefalu, Sicily, we found a very modest motel that would accommodate us without reservations. Our room, not much bigger than an SUV, was perched right above the expansive sea. The ocean, I have come to realize, is my soul connection to the world. Everything about the entire picture speaks to me, calms me. I had never seen this particular water before, but I loved the Mediterranean immediately, with its dark strength, a masculine, midnight blue. The waves didn't dance and shake like the exotic whipped-up waters of the Gulf; they rolled and murmured as if simmering in a great cauldron.

That same day, Steve bought me our first Sicilian souvenir—a floppy straw hat—on our walk down to the water. In a matter of moments, we were in the deep, dark blue, new straw hat and sunscreen back on the shore. The water was cold and expansive, and it momentarily washed off the dirt of the Middle East.

We raced out to a rock that jutted up twenty feet from the surface of the ocean. Steve swims like a fish, and I couldn't keep up with him as he cut through the water. I paddled after him awkwardly, trying to catch my breath from the shock of the temperature. Almost instantly, he was yelling at me from the top of the rock. He had shimmied his way up the slick algae and was raising his arms and calling out for me to "Hurry, Hurry!" like a little boy playing king of the mountain.

I kept paddling until I was at the base of the rock and somehow managed to climb up next to him. "Now let's jump!" he said, which is what I knew he was going to say. I knew I didn't want to jump, though for some reason I had crawled up that rock anyway. "Here, watch!" he said as he sailed through the air. He hit the water, submerged, resurfaced, and shouted up to me, "It's safe. Jump to me. You can do it!" His big green eyes were lit up like a traffic signal saying "Go!"

I was frozen with fear. I wasn't scared to die or worried I would get hurt or afraid of hitting the water. I was desperately afraid of what it would feel like to fall, and I couldn't will myself to launch off the safety of the rock.

After some coaching and coaxing and reassuring, I finally stepped off the rock — not really a full-fledged jump — into total nothingness, and I raced down toward Steve's voice. As much as I didn't want to jump, more than that, I didn't want to be ruled by fear. I wanted to be free and courageous, which often means doing something in spite of how scary it feels.

I was terrified as I fell, but it only lasted a split second, and then I plunged into the water and surfaced right beside Steve, gasping and choking and realigning my skewed bathing suit. I felt breathless and wild with the excitement of the free fall. The risk killed fear's power, and I was — for one brief second — brave.

Steve was exultant and slapped the water as he congratulated me on my flight. And just like that, he was off, gliding through the water with his own version of grace. I paddled after him,

found art

feeling the water on my skin as my heart pounded all the way to the shore.

When we returned from Sicily, the Navy paid for us to live in a hotel for a week while we transitioned. We locked the door at Starview, turned in our key to Mr. Sharif, and headed for the Novatel. We enjoyed the last of the oppressive July heat poolside at the hotel.

Those days of waiting to leave Bahrain were full of mixed emotions. We visited the *souq* for the last time, enjoyed a good-bye brioche at Café Lilou, consumed our weight in *shawarmas* one last time, hugged the friends we had made, said good-bye to Yousef at Khazana, gave Steve's bike to the Nepalese watchman at Starview—who acted as though we had given him our firstborn (Mohammed was insanely jealous)—and with just a few hours before our flight took off, we finally managed to sell our car. Our affairs were in order to leave, but saying good-bye would be a much longer process.

I was very alive then. My skin was tan, my appetite was hearty, my body was fit, and my soul and spirit were present and palpable. I was aware of myself in the world, and I was aware of the world in myself, both of which are so rare. The cumulative effect of the year had left me healthy, but, truthfully, I was isolated. I knew I couldn't just stay that way for the rest of my life (as appealing as the prospect was). I had to return to "real life."

As we sat at the Novatel, waiting to leave Bahrain and return to the States, I felt the same way I felt when I peered off the edge of that wet rock in Sicily—alive and very scared. The minute I climbed up the rock I knew that my only choice in getting down was to jump. The mass of algae was far too slick and the pitch of the rock far too steep to try to slide down the sides. I'm not sure I had thought this all the way through when I came to Bahrain. Inevitably I'd have to jump back into the swirling waters of real life, and there would be no easing into it. In addition, I hadn't counted on how frightening the jumping would be.

I was unsure how to take this person I had become and integrate it with the person I had been and with the life waiting for me in San Diego. I had no idea how I was going to assimilate the God-moments of Bahrain into the increased responsibilities and tasks I would no doubt be returning to. I had no idea how I would sustain the revelations I had been given.

For those few nights, we were absolutely between worlds. One foot was still standing on the sure footing of Bahrain, and the other was stepping toward an ironically foreign unknown — and an entire ocean stretched beneath us. The voices of fear began clamoring once again, and I knew the only way to silence them was to step out into the very thing I wanted to avoid. I looked down and out — the water and the shore both looking far away and small — and I longed to be brave.

20

weeping

Soon after we arrived in San Diego, a woman's group asked me if I would come and speak to them about my time in Bahrain. I agonized over what to talk about, trying so hard to make sense of my Middle Eastern experiences and bring some truth or insight to these women that they could translate into their own lives.

In preparation for the talk, I thought specifically about that moment in the Starview kitchen and the call to prayer. I thought about Fatima and the mosque and how much I wanted to go back and sit in the middle of the inner courtyard in a borrowed *abaya*. I thought about the moment I stood between Mega Mart and the meat market, and I thought about Nawal's villa.

I scanned my Bahrain journal for talking points and ideas, and I made a list of a few different kicky stories I could share. But the core of me was overwhelmed with being back home and trying to process all that I had seen and heard, and I couldn't figure out what I *really* wanted to say about Bahrain. Instead, I began to cry.

I begged God for words and insight and courage. I pleaded with myself to get to work and come up with something valuable and brilliant. I chastised the universe for making me feel so lost and unmoored. All of this erupted through bitter tears, and I wished I could just hop on a plane and return to the land where I was expected to produce nothing.

Two nights before the event, I was coming apart at the seams. I had no real "message" yet, and the panic was bubbling up inside me like liver bile burning a hole in my throat. I remember praying—a literal prayer to God—that I would get in a car accident and be put in the hospital so I wouldn't have to speak at the event.

I called my mom and told her I was on my way to her house for help. I bawled the entire stretch of freeway from my house to hers and made a couple emergency phone calls to friends begging for prayer. My friend Tina assured me I was capable of putting the talk together and prayed for me over the phone as I drove and sobbed. As soon as she uttered the amen, she proceeded to yell at me for driving in such a state and made me promise to put the phone away until I got to my mom's.

The silence inside the car gave me more opportunity for self-inspection, and by the time I pulled into the familiar cul-de-sac, I was unceremoniously ripping myself a new one. *They just want you to get up there and talk about living in the Middle East. It's not like there's a wrong answer. How hard is it?* I badgered.

Turns out, it was really, really hard.

My mom helped me organize my thoughts, and a phone call with my mother-in-law also helped provide some clarity. Enough that I could get up in front of a roomful of women and say something that made sense and mattered.

After the event was over, my friend Linsey—who often knows me better than I know myself—said, "That's the most serious I've ever seen you when you're speaking."

I've never forgotten that comment. She was right. I was stern and sad.

Publicly speaking about Bahrain felt like I was giving the eulogy at the funeral of someone I dearly loved. I was no longer in the midst of this great experience. I was now speaking about it as a past memory.

I never thought saying good-bye would be so hard. Probably because I never, in my wildest dreams, thought that year would be so profound. The transformative powers of the desert (aka God) caught me completely off guard, and that made the foreign place all the more beautiful and mysterious.

"Why does it always make you cry?" Linsey asked me.

No matter where I was or what I was doing or who I was with, if the topic of Bahrain came up, my eyes would immediately fill up with tears, to the point that my knee-jerk emotions became so predictable that we would all just laugh the minute I would start to cry. You could set your watch by the tears.

I found a Scripture recently that explains the whole phenomenon. I wish I would have had such wisdom then, when I was struggling to understand the deep significance of my experiences.

> I will give you the treasures of darkness,
>   riches stored in secret places,
> so that you may know that I am the LORD,
>   the God of Israel, who summons you by name.
>
> Isaiah 45:3

Coming back from somewhere significant — a pilgrimage of any kind — is personal, particular, and often lonely. The treasures and riches of such a journey are locked away, and though we may know that something is down there somewhere, the truth is hard to access and make sense of.

The truth of Bahrain, the meaning behind the experience, was locked away deep inside me. I kept Ecclesiastes 3 in front of me to help me cope, "He has made everything beautiful in its time ... yet no one can fathom what God has done from beginning to end." That Scripture has become a mantra for me since.

Slowly and surely, he has given me the treasures and the riches. He has helped me make sense of that time and myself in that place. He has shown me how Bahrain was a reclamation on so many levels and how I can bring that reclaimed self into today and tomorrow.

Like my very own Red Sea, Bahrain was a place of passage—out of slavery and into freedom. For one magical year, the seas parted and invisible wall-hands suspended the agitated seas, and I was able to walk around on dry ground.

Of course, none of this was clear to me upon returning. All I could see and feel was the swirling mess of the waters that had somehow crashed back in on me when I wasn't looking.

The only thing harder than going to Bahrain was coming home. *I can't really go back*, I wrote in my journal and then underlined. *I sit here trying to go back so I can go forward again. But I know I can't really go back.*

Cue the tears.

21

planting

Last year, my friend Corrie rented a house with a small flower box out front. The planter was incredibly desolate, so she went about the task of refurbishing the soil in an attempt to plant some strawberries. Along the way, earthworms were beheaded, weeds were hacked up and untangled, and dirt was displaced. All this before a single strawberry could go in the ground.

Cultivating earth for new roots is the dirtiest of work, and I knew this before I ever got back to San Diego. Investing in the soil once again takes commitment and effort, none of which I had ample supply of after expending such great energy to plant myself in Bahrain. There I was, waiting for the promised strawberries to come forth yet again.

To further complicate matters, Steve began traveling right after we touched down in San Diego. We were told his job would be a relatively uneventful desk job. That lasted about five minutes. Welcome to the Navy! They called his number and invited him to oversee a Task Unit—a great opportunity for him and a huge liability for us. All of a sudden, Steve was in and out constantly with workups.

Workups are the pre-deployment purgatory when the Task Unit (made up of two SEAL platoons) takes innumerable forays all over God's green earth—and God's desolate desert earth, too—for training purposes. This is the preparation before the main event (the deployment), and the trips are endless, usually entailing about twelve to eighteen months of shooting every imaginable weapon while preparing for special operations in every imaginable terrain—from the desert to the mountains to the water. Most wives will tell you that deployment is a relief after workups. At least then something is constant.

Steve would sometimes travel to three countries during a one-week trip, and if we were lucky, his Task Unit was home about half the month. Just as soon as we fell into any sort of rhythm at all, he was out the door again.

This required us to grit our teeth and do our best to stay married and endure the revolving door that our relationship had been reduced to. Staying connected was difficult because the communication options were usually minimal.

Doing life well feels virtually impossible when you have little idea what the next week holds. I couldn't see past the pile of dusty, desert-camouflaged backpacks that constantly lined our hallway, and we were forced into surviving.

We were learning to do marriage all over again in *this* new place, with all of its demands. Some days we handled our new life well, communicating our way through the maze of people, travel, and responsibilities. Other days, we bombed. Badly.

I longed for even just a hint of the ripened summer fruit, but none could be found on first glance.

Planting, like writing, losing weight, or remodeling a kitchen, is a process. A shortcut to growth does not exist. I had to decide if I would trust the process or not—and then I remembered the Tree of Life.

South of the Grand Mosque, out in the-middle-of-nowhere-

Bahrain, you'll find a tourist destination called the Tree of Life. The climate is temperamental and fussy in this region of the island, and when I first made the drive out to visit the renowned tree, my hair whipped me in the face and my clothes snapped like a sail.

The whole scene wasn't much to look at, if you ask me. Everything was the blah desert beige of rocks and sand. Oil pipelines snaked across the dry ground here and there, but the black tubing was the only interruption in an otherwise monotone landscape. That is, except for the Tree of Life.

Legend has it that the Tree of Life, a four-hundred-year-old mesquite, is the only tree in all of Bahrain that grows from natural irrigation. Though surrounded by barren nothingness, this one huge tree shoots up, green and leafy and alive.

The tree is a monument to the unexpected art of Creator God. Even in the most desperate places, even in the most desolate deserts, even in the most foreign of soils, something beautiful can and will grow.

I did my best to believe—yet again—despite my unbelief that the awkward plucking had intention and that the soil would produce some delicious strawberries if I could bear to invest in its nutritive essence one more time. The tending and trusting didn't make anything miraculously easier, frankly. But they did remind me that, though I had a part in the planting process, the production of fruit wasn't all up to me. This was an important lesson I had learned once before in a very sacred place.

a navy seal trident

22
mourning

Once the seemingly endless months of workups were completed, Steve climbed onto a plane bound for Africa, and four months later he stepped off, back in San Diego. Our friends and I gathered at the airport with signs and cameras and welcomed him home with our own homespun fanfare.

Steve's first night back we went straight to a rooftop restaurant and sat for hours, talking about all the things we couldn't discuss while he was away. Balmy and breezy, the night air wrapped around us, and I remember Steve looking Middle Eastern tan in his white linen shirt. We toasted togetherness, talking in our own little world. The moment was magical and fleeting.

On another rooftop, a world away, tragedy was unfolding.

With bags barely unpacked and the African sand just washed from his uniform, Steve received a phone call. The call came in the middle of the night, which, as you know, is the worst kind of call to receive. There had been an incident involving SEALs in downtown Ramadie, Iraq, and Steve was to go directly to the base office for more details.

At his office, Steve was notified of three casualties — two injured, one killed. Ramadie was one of the most dangerous hot zones in Iraq during those dog days of the war, and this particular platoon was caught in a rooftop gunfight that ended badly. One of the injured SEALs was an officer around Steve's age who had been shot in the back. Luckily, the bullet lodged in his body armor, and he was able to return to combat right away. The other injured SEAL was shot in the face and was medically evacuated for treatment. Though his life was saved, he was left blinded in both eyes, completely losing his right eye.

The third casualty was a twenty-eight-year-old SEAL whom Steve had trained with throughout workups the previous year. Marc was shot and killed while providing protection for his fellow teammates as they were evacuating the two wounded men. Marc was the first SEAL to die in Iraq and would posthumously be awarded the Silver Star for his bravery.

By nine o'clock the next morning Steve was on a plane to New York—not home two weeks from deployment himself—to go meet Marc's widow, Maya. The Navy assigned Steve to be her liaison, walking with her from just hours after she found out about her husband's death through the first few weeks of the grief and the innumerable decisions and logistics that needed attending to.

Steve called me a couple times while he was in New York to say things like, "You know I love you, right? You know I really love you." And I would say, "I know, honey. I know you do."

I will never know exactly what happened those weeks while Steve was in New York. I will never know what it was like for him to be with Maya and her family in the middle of such a nightmare. I will never understand how he internalized the experience of helping someone cope with such a great loss. But I do know that it all still sits deeply with him. He still carries those days with him, and maybe he always will.

After his trip to New York, Steve escorted Maya and her mother back to San Diego. Marc was buried at Fort Rosecrans National Cemetery in San Diego. The cemetery, with its eternal rows of white headstones, overlooks the Pacific Ocean on one side and the SEAL training facility, BUD/S, on the other.

Steve sat beside Maya as her official escort on the day she laid her husband to rest. It was the saddest day I can remember. The wind of it still whispers through our house. Hot sun burned my chest red as we sat in the August heat perched atop Point Loma, high above the San Diego harbor, looking out onto the ocean. We sat in rows of wooden folding chairs set up between the graves. The sight of it all is suffocating, every headstone a father, son, or brother, a mother, sister, or daughter. Each with his or her own story of life and death.

Everyone spoke in a dull hum as awkward pleasantries were exchanged. Uniformed SEALs, those who were not deployed, milled around greeting each other and kissing wives and girlfriends. Dignitaries, admirals, and Navy brass mingled in and around the rank and file. Death, as they say, was so clearly the great equalizer.

Seated in front of a large portrait of Marc and huge sprays of flowers, we waited for the black Suburban to arrive. Military boys with quivering chins brought the casket to the front as bagpipers breathed "Amazing Grace." The next Suburban arrived, and my handsome husband in his Service Dress Blues emerged, extending his hand for Maya, who stepped out in a black halter dress with a flowing skirt. Dark red rigatoni ringlets framed her large sunglasses. She grasped Steve's arm as they made their way to the front row. A widow at twenty-five.

An officer knelt down in front of Maya and presented her with the flag from Marc's casket. "On behalf of a grateful nation ...," he began, reciting the words no woman would ever want to hear.

As the funeral concluded, the immediate family members and their Navy escorts recessed on foot, walking down the center aisle, up an adjacent hill, to the burial plot. I watched Steve and Maya, arm in arm, slowly walk behind the hearse. Family members and other uniformed escorts followed Steve and Maya, and the procession ended with the bagpipers.

They inched up the hill until they were completely out of sight. Later, Steve told me that the SEALs present at the grave each took turns pushing a Trident (the SEAL insignia) pin into the side of Marc's casket. Before it was lowered into the ground, Steve knelt down next to Maya as she said her final words to Marc, whispering their song to him as her good-bye.

I cried the entire day. I cried from a place that was deep and mysterious even to me. I cried for Maya. I cried for the future they had been robbed of, the children they had been refused, the wretched tragedy of a life cut so terribly short. I cried for the war and the many, like Maya, who have lost so enormously. I cried for myself and for Steve and for all the times I had feared that it would be my door they would knock on and his name they would speak. I cried because Steve had been spared, and I couldn't understand why Marc had not. I cried because God seemed absent and cold in my fear and grief and worry, like he was cruel and cryptic. I cried the entire day of Marc's funeral, and for countless days after — every day — as though my heart was being squeezed with the huge, heavy hand of grief.

After Steve put Maya back on the plane for New York, we decided to go to the beach for the weekend to decompress and to commemorate our anniversary, which had come and gone in the middle of the previous week. The morning after we arrived at our dive hotel with the all-hours nightclub next door (all we could find online so last-minute), Steve received another phone call from the base. This time, Steve would be going to Iraq.

We hurried home on Sunday, spent Monday packing, and by Tuesday morning he was on a plane headed to Baghdad, where he would catch a helicopter to Fallujah. I don't think it had even been a week since Marc's funeral when we received the call that Steve would be going. Our insides were still skinned and splayed open.

I held my breath the entire time Steve was in Iraq. I sat with a fearful ache for those two months—numb and terrorized all at the same time. I don't even remember the day he returned. I just remember that at some point we were living together again.

In the end, Steve was gone about ten months out of that year. During the time he was home, we celebrated the holidays, we traveled to see family, our lives became connected with a young woman named Maya, and we buried a teammate—not the first and not the last. It has been some time now since many of those events took place, and I'm not sure we have moved past them or that we ever will. How can we?

From Maya, I have learned the importance of walking into grief—as foreign as it often feels—of acknowledging and allowing in its severe presence.

Steve and I met with Maya every few months after Marc's death when she was in San Diego settling a seemingly endless list of affairs. Over brunch or sushi or coffee downtown, I watched her sit in her pain, month after month. It seemed impossible that the cloud of grief would ever lift. Yet I could glimpse in Maya what it might be like to mourn deeply in such a way that the loss would always be present, and yet, would also have a sense of great beauty—the beauty of someone who had allowed themselves to walk into their pain.

We paid our respects to Marc—our limitless and profound respects. His death affected each and every one of us uniquely:

SEAL Team Three has been in existence for over twenty-five years and had never lost a single SEAL until Marc's death. Because most of the Team was deployed at that time, many of Marc's teammates and friends weren't even able to attend his funeral. I found the lack of closure a cruelty for those boys, among the many other difficult burdens they were carrying. The younger, wide-eyed SEALs who attended the funeral—many of whom had just finished BUD/S and reported to a Team—mourned whatever notions of romance war still carried for them. Maya mourned the great loss of her husband. I mourned the loss of mine.

On that hot morning at Fort Rosecrans, I faced my greatest fear. I was Abraham preparing the altar for Isaac, and the burden was impossible. Why would God ask for the most precious thing? Why would he attach such great vulnerability and risk to the purity of love? I had to let go of Steve that day. After spending so much of our relationship holding as tightly as I possibly could, I felt angry and crazed and desperately sad to have to relinquish him.

Marc's death spoke to the utter lack of assurances life offers us. No matter how much I believed in and trusted God, no matter how spiritual I was, no matter how much I prayed on Steve's behalf, I had no guarantees that God would spare my husband. I realized my sense of entitlement when it came to Steve's life—that I felt I was owed it. Letting go of that notion was nothing but pain.

Pain, like no other place perhaps, is where our art is born,

found art

where our stories are written, our canvases brushed, our scores composed. Though we so often want to deny the discomfort, suffering is one of the few things that can lead us to the place where we find the God we so desperately long for.

Yes, even though we walk through the valley of the shadow of death, he is with us. In our greatest need, he sees us.

A long bridge spans over the San Diego Bay. I take that bridge every day to get to my house from the mainland of San Diego. At the crest of the bridge you can see panoramic views up and down the coast. On clear days you can see all the way out to the horizon, where the Coronado Islands bump up out of the Pacific Ocean like huge floating rocks. To the south, you can see Tijuana, Mexico, congested and close. To the north, you can see the long jutting peninsula of Point Loma, where Marc is buried.

Grief has a way of staying with us, of never letting us forget. Maybe not as acute as the first day we felt it—wild, untamed, beastly—but no less present in its duller and daily state.

When we cross over the bridge and see the sun backlighting Point Loma against the silvery water, we think about Marc. And, truthfully, I also think about Steve.

23

hating

After Marc was killed, I went through another tailspin concerning the war. I thought of the anger I felt in Bahrain when we got the news that four Navy boys from our base had been killed, and all the conflictedness of that time reared up in me with a vengeance.

A base is a juxtaposed world of honor and daily duty, where people go about the business of fighting terrorism during the day and then go home and eat dinner with their families at night. The war coexists with the everyday. Uniformed gunmen walk the same sidewalks as overheated mothers and surly children. War heroes take aerobics classes and buy pregnancy tests. Admirals and civilians share a pew in the chapel. Distracted wives step aside while routine car searches are conducted for explosives at the base gate. Heightened security, top-secret deployments, and machine guns become as daily as day care and dentist appointments.

As soon as our lives would strike a bit of everydayness, the losses — coming in waves one right after another — had a way of reminding us why we were all really there together. Death was everywhere, living among us like a shadow. Just when we'd forgotten, just when we'd been able to focus on ordinary life, tragedy would strike yet again.

Nothing cut through the normalcy like news from the front lines. I remember the day Steve came home from work around 7:30 or so. No sooner had we eaten dinner than his phone rang. Due to the nature of his job, this was never out of the ordinary, but I could tell by the look on his face that the news he was receiving was not good.

He ended the call and went back to work. When he finally returned home, four or five hours later, I learned that earlier in the day a rogue boat in the Persian Gulf exploded just as a U.S. Navy boat was approaching it — a floating, improvised explosive device. Three U.S. servicemen died immediately, and one was flown to Germany, where he later died.

Within a couple of days, pictures of these four boys in their dress uniforms covered the front page of the base newspaper. My stomach turned when I saw them looking out at me from the headlines, all so baby-faced and handsome. I wondered, neither for the first or the last time, what it must be like to bury someone so young and full of promise.

I was seething from the senselessness and permanency. I tried to pick up the paper and read the story, but I would see the faces of the four boys and immediately put the paper down again. I couldn't bring myself to read about their lives, their jobs, those they left behind. I was already far too close to them, and I couldn't afford to get any closer. Every time I passed a newsstand on base, I turned the paper over so the faces were hidden. Maybe that isn't honoring the dead. I don't know.

I am ever tempted to hate this war. I walk such an imperceptibly fine line of believing in our cause in Iraq and Afghanistan and yet desperately hating the cost it requires.

Sometimes that line becomes very blurred in my head. On those days, I feel far too young to be facing these circumstances. I feel too young to be writing history with the lives of my peers. I want to throw parties with festive food and lively music and not worry about the rest of the world. I want to be as frivolous and fancy and unburdened as youth should be. Yet the unwavering iron anchor attached to my soul makes me feel old and grave.

I recently saw a magazine photograph of the golden ends of six ammunition casings upright in an ammunition pouch, not yet loaded into a weapon. On the ends of each casing was a handwritten message in black marker: 4 Doug, 4 Taryn, 4 Mom, FREE, 9 – 11. The soldiers had named their rounds before entering combat, reminding themselves of what they were fighting for. The magazine article, "Another Forgotten War?" told the story of an Army platoon stationed in the Korengal Valley — "some of Afghanistan's deadliest acreage," it reported.

Just looking at the pictures made me sweaty and riled. The seething sadness raged up in me, and I felt like I was going to choke on my anger. I can't believe this is our world.

We live in a world where young soldiers sit between life and death and fire rounds of ammunition at the enemy with their mothers' names handwritten on it. We live in a world where stray bullets kill young SEALs, where youth feels complicated, where hope flickers very dimly, where children cannot attend school, where some do not eat, where women are silenced, where churches discriminate, where anxiety steals lives, where perfectionism is worshiped, where differences are mocked. We live in a world shot through with injustice. This is depressing and angering and crazy-making.

I was at the Seef Mall Starbucks drinking a latte one day. A huge crowd started gathering around a giant man. Literally, he was at least eight feet tall and looked like Andre the Giant in the face, which made me think he was suffering from one of those pituitary diseases that caused him to be so big. He seemed almost as tall as the entire escalator he was standing in front of. I noticed that his eyes were vacant.

His "handler" was collecting money from anyone who wanted a picture taken with him. "Your hands next to his hands, your feet next to his feet, your head next to his head. Step right up." Everyone was mad with excitement, waving money at the handler. The giant never said a word, and his empty expression never changed.

I wanted to scream out at the cruelty of the scene, but I just sat across the way, drinking my latte with tears in my eyes and a hot ire stirring in my gut. In the end, I did nothing, because there was nothing I could do. I felt as impotent as that giant man standing in the Seef Mall and looking like a circus animal.

This is how I feel about the war — and the other injustices of the world — just about every day. Like all I can do is sit back and watch things fall apart while I drown my sorrows at Starbucks. I hate that the world is cruel, and I hate that I feel powerless against the brutality.

The options, as I see it, are to act as if none of this is happening; acknowledge what is happening but act as if it has no effect on me; live in total, hopeless devastation due to the state of the world; or look for God.

All of these options have consequences. Gloom and doom and denial are tempting, but on closer inspection I realize they are just a cop-out. Living a lifeless dirge may seem like the responsible and appropriate thing to do, but in the end, I think pessimism is even more self-consumed and empty than denial.

Living in reality is actually very hard. Looking for God, in what seems like the most godless reality, is probably the hardest yet. My fear in looking for him is that I will find a God I don't agree with or understand. How could I possibly reconcile this war with believing in sweet and loving Jesus? Let me tell you, the theology feels nearly impossible. I have had to mount great courage in order to keep believing despite my anger, disgust, and disillusionment.

The war has asked an impossible amount from so many. It has asked us to relinquish husbands, wives, brothers, sisters, sons, daughters, mothers, and fathers. It has asked us to sit and listen to the many voices who comment so knowingly on a life they have never experienced. It has asked us to come to terms with the costs associated with such an enormous cause, and for some, it has been an inestimable cost. Beyond all other burdens, the war has left us with the inordinate task of grieving the death of our youth. This is the most unnatural and incomprehensible grief to bear.

Where is God in such loss? Where is God while the world is splitting at the seams? I have shaken my fist at him a time or two and asked him what he could possibly be thinking.

I have watched young widows grieve — Maya and others — and such tragedy is just about the worst thing to witness in this world. I have seen soldiers, sailors, and Marines weep bitterly for the loss of their brothers and sisters in combat. I have shared a sidewalk with a young uniformed boy one week and read about his death the next. I have sat in the stabbing fear of possible loss myself. But I have never stopped believing that God was there. I cannot perfectly reconcile the horrible injustice in this world with the love of God. I don't have the right answer to such a dilemma that would, once and for all, quiet such questions.

Here's what I do know: Despite their grief, I have watched

young widows survive. Despite their anger, I have watched soldiers heal with time. Despite my fear, I trust again. These are the places where I see God. We are able to go on—not in the ways we might have if this war would have never happened, but we are able to love again and trust again and believe again and breathe again. That is God, for I know I am incapable of these mighty efforts on my own.

I have so few answers when it comes to the theology of war. Most days, I just feel full of sadness and then rage. I hate that our world is so terribly messed up, and it seems as though the innocent and the young are constantly paying the price. In the face of the world's cruelties—and they are plenty and varied and ever upsetting—I will choose to hate the injustice. I will choose to look for God, even if he is hiding in the smallest fold or the slightest crease, because I know in the very deepest parts of me, undoubtedly, he is there.

a receipt from the russian-georgian
restaurant on louisiana street

24

breaking down

My church called and offered me a part-time job working with married couples, which was funny because I had only been married a year. When you go to a young church, a year is a lifetime apparently. I was assured I had more than enough credentials to do the job. Also, churches need willing people, not always expert people. I was willing.

I accepted, and within minutes I had the emotional equivalent of hives. I had summarily gone from the annals of a desert monastery to the set of *High School Musical*. Swarms of young, impossibly hip, fashion-savvy people—who loved God, no less—were everywhere. Who were all these pretty, spiritual people with their faux hawks and skinny jeans?

Many of the familiar faces I remembered from before Bahrain were now gone. New, unfamiliar faces had taken their place. I was confronted by an inconvenient truth: I had to start all over.

The only thing I could think to do was to throw a tantrum internally and become incredibly territorial and wish away all these new people. So Christlike. I just couldn't see how I would ever get comfortable in a church full of foreigners.

I decided the best thing to do was hide. After all, Jesus hid a time or two, right?

"I think I'm an introvert," I told Linsey (who also worked at the church) on a particularly overwhelming day. She laughed out loud and said, "What's wrong?" knowing I had never been introverted a day in my life.

"I just don't know what to do with all these people in my life."

"Yeah," she said, "that's community."

I soon realized that hiding was a flawed plan. A member of a church staff can't very well isolate herself from the church attendees while trying to conduct "ministry." The fly in the ointment is that ministry is a bit of a hands-on job. There went that strategy.

Painstakingly, I went about the agonizing task of assimilating. I joined a group, I met with handfuls of women for coffee, Steve and I invited all sorts of people over for dinner, and I tried to be generally available. To be completely truthful, most all of the time, I felt exhausted from these efforts. I carried the burden of knowing I had changed—of feeling like an outsider and even misunderstood at times—and that was about all I had energy to do.

One night at church, I watched a girl with long black hair dance across the stage to a Coldplay song.* I didn't know the girl then, though she would become a sister to me later on. I didn't know the song either, as I'd been holed up and spectacularly removed from American pop culture.

And the tears come streaming down your face
when you lose something you can't replace

---

*Coldplay, "Fix You" (September 2005); lyrics by Guy Berryman, Will Champion, Chris Martin, and Jon Buckland.

I sat in the back of the huge gym where our church was meeting at the time. I was so far back that I could see the heads of a thousand people in front of me and then the stage.

Tears did come streaming down my face as I watched Erica float across the stage, her outline projected onto the walls like a hundred fireflies flitting around the ceiling. I felt like the song was for me, and the whole evening a salve for the raw places inside me.

Then I heard a couple of sniffles around me, and I realized that the entire room was collectively leaning forward. It hit me that everyone in the gym felt like that song was for them. Everyone was carrying something. I had been too busy focusing on my own losses to realize that I wasn't the only one in need.

Coldplay got it right. We all feel tired, stuck in reverse, like we've tried and failed, like we've lost something irreplaceable. All of us have wondered if it could be worse. We each long to be fixed and guided home.

In an instant, I felt surrounded and known and among friends. Even if I didn't know these people as acquaintances, I knew them on a level deeper than coffee dates and dinner parties. I knew their souls. We were all in that gym for the same reason. We needed God, and we needed each other.

I remember an ancient Islamic prayer tradition that Fatima told me about when I was touring the Grand Mosque. In Islam, the worshipers come to the mosque five times a day — gathered as strangers — to pray. The tradition calls worshipers to stand shoulder to shoulder and foot to foot with each other, creating one continuous line, like a row of paper dolls all across the prayer hall. In a symbolic gesture of solidarity, each person widens their stance so that his or her bare feet are touching the bare feet of the person on either side.

As the prayers are offered, the worshiper is no longer simply one person, isolated and individualized, though they are one person still. He or she also becomes part of the larger body, praying together in unison.

In the gym at my church, I felt the warm presence of my community. *My* community. Imperfect strangers—who are all a little crazy, might I add—standing together to worship and be healed, shoulder to shoulder and foot to foot. How gloriously beautiful is the body of Christ.

The resistance in me began to break down like a spring thaw.

25

turning away

I started meeting with a woman who was skilled at listening and being a companion and praying. I was still having trouble managing without some help, and she was help in the best sense of the word. As soon as I smelled the upholstery in her office, I started crying. We met for two hours once a month, and I talked the entire time. She listened to my wild rants, teary streaks, and emotional confessions as if I were offering the most coherent thoughts.

I confessed that I watched *Dawson's Creek* reruns at nine in the morning with a spoonful of peanut butter in one hand and a Diet Coke in the other. I also confided in her that I let my phone ring and ring until the voice mail was completely filled up. I admitted that I wanted to hide out a lot. I told her how free I felt in Bahrain and how utterly pent-up I was feeling back in the States.

To all this, she just nodded in a very validating sort of way. She gave me permission to wallow a bit—a very little bit—and she also gave me direction on how to reach into the places that were sad and weepy. When I met with her, I felt like at least one person in the world knew how very badly off I was but still believed I could make it.

"I feel like I'm a fake," I told her at one of our meetings. She wrote down the phrase on this huge sheet of white paper hanging on an easel. She had a knack for writing down certain words or phrases I said. I think she wanted me to really look at the stuff that was going on in my head and not just let it bounce around the room unattended. I always took these papers with me when we were done. I didn't do anything special with them. I just folded them up and put them in the bottom shelf of my bookcase so I could see the creases and edges and know I was moving toward something, despite how ugly things seemed to feel.

"I'm trying to figure out who I am now, and nothing I do or say feels right." I wasn't sure what other people wanted from me, and I wasn't sure what I wanted from myself. I just felt like I was doing things wrong or badly quite often, and that everyone was noticing. The more I tried to posture and perform and manage, the farther I felt from myself and the more I felt like a fraud—and all of this combined to press Play on the thousands of hours of toxic tapes in my head that told me I was flawed and unworthy.

The deeply disappointing thing about all this was that I had been so sure all of these ugly parts of me had been completely lobotomized in Bahrain. The reality was, transformation takes so much time, and the major shifts had just begun. Bahrain was the detox. Now the time had come for rehab.

I see "I feel like a fake" at the top of the white paper, and I can't stop staring at it. Just one little sentence, but these five words are keeping me locked in some sort of impossibly small cage.

"Well, are you?" she asks.

I sit and look at her in silence like this moment is the first

found art

time I have ever thought to stand up to the voices feeding me so much BS about myself. It never occurred to me to question what I was hearing inside my head or to entertain the fact that the voices could be wrong. I just agreed. As much as the voices had been feeding me, I was also feeding them. I had been offering nourishing hunks of myself to chew on every day, cannibalizing myself for absolutely no good reason at all.

"Leeana, are you? Are you a fake?" she asks again because I was staring off in silence.

"No. No, I am not a fake," I finally answer with conviction, after taking some time to really think and consider the truth.

We closed out our two hours with prayer. I longed to turn away from the lies, but the truth was hard to believe. I tried the best I could to admit my reluctance out loud to God and to her and to myself.

We agreed to spend our next few times together talking through some of the specific tapes that were playing in my head. For months, literally months, I stepped into the darkness only long enough to turn on some light.

Every month, I walked away with another folded white paper under my arm. I now have stacks of these papers stuffed into the bottom of my bookcase. Here is what they say:

- I am capable and smart, but I am not quite enough.
- I can't be wrong because then people will see I am flawed.
- Everything I do is an effort to get people to notice me.
- Who do I think I am?
- Why did I just say that?
- Why am I trying so hard right now?
- What does that person think of me?
- I have good things to offer, but I'm not [insert the name of

any person who seems to be just a bit more together than me in any or all areas].
- People can see through me.
- I am going to fail.

The work was terrible, I won't lie. Confronting the deepest secrets and worst thoughts about ourselves is exhausting. In the midst of all the soul-searching, I missed Bahrain even more completely. In Bahrain, I had so much space and so few expectations placed on me. I had no one to impress. No one to disappoint.

Realizing I wouldn't and couldn't return, I did my very best to capture the essence of Bahrain — what had made me feel free and alive — and I tried to put those words down on paper as well, so I could infuse even just one minute of my day with such necessities as beauty, space, silence, sweating, candles, reflecting, observing, creating, loving. Out of these simple beats, I began constructing my new rhythm.

26

speaking

I have a group of girls I meet with every Monday night. They are a lifeline. More than they know, probably. I suspect, though, that each of us is a lifeline for the other.

After we had been meeting for just a few months, we went to the Russian-Georgian restaurant on the corner of Louisiana Street (of course). It's the kind of restaurant where you write all over the walls and eat cherry soup and sip Turkish coffee after letting the owner order your entire dinner for you.

We were there for the food, the company, and the piano, which sits right out in the middle of the restaurant unattended — except for the Monday nights when my group visits. We always goad Wanida to play and sing for us. Wanida is the one with the insane voice. Not just lovely or nice, but inspired.

This particular night, she acted timid and modest and uncomfortable as she pushed back her chair and headed toward the middle of the room sheepishly. She perched herself on the edge of the old bench and began to play "Amazing Grace" — softly and sweetly at first, background music, as if she were afraid people might hear her. But before long, the music began coming from a deeper place in Wanida. She bowed and swayed, her back rounded over the keys as she went somewhere beyond Louisiana Street.

Spontaneously, people ducked in off the streets, dishwashers emerged from the kitchen, and the owner stood up from his seat in the corner — all to listen to Wanida.

"You must sing," the owner gushed when she was done with the song. "Really. Really. You must *do* something with the voice."

We explained to him that Wanida sang at our church most Sundays, and that hundreds of people were blessed by her every week. But he wasn't satisfied.

"No. No. Not enough! The *world* needs to hear the voice." He kept pushing. Why hadn't she done some recording? Why doesn't she sing professionally? Why had no one discovered her? Wanida smiled graciously through her discomfort — not the first time she'd been subject to such a barrage of expectations.

I don't think it has always been easy for Wanida to have this voice. Some people can't seem to get past their shock or insecurity or envy, and so a gift such as hers can feel more like a liability than an asset. I wonder if Wanida feels the freedom to let herself be really big, to be as big as the voice God has given her. I wonder if she's afraid of what it might cost if she fully embraces it.

Our group went back to the restaurant almost a year later. The inside felt smaller and safer than I had remembered. Wanida sang again. This time she sang her own songs — songs she had written over the last year. She sang her very own words with her very own voice. No one came off the street to listen. No dishwashers came out of the kitchen. No patrons perked up from their tables. One lone waiter sat in the corner table closest to the kitchen. The owner sat in the exact same spot he was sitting the last time we were there.

This time, he just listened. "It was a pleasure," the owner said. And that was all he said.

Writing her own songs was an act of bravery on Wanida's part—and singing them to us was as well.

Coming home from Bahrain, I longed to be small and unnoticed and reclusive. I was afraid of failing if I spoke up. I was afraid of the expectations and the energy that would need to be expended if I were to say anything at all.

One day I was out walking during some free time at a conference I was attending. Making my way aimlessly through a field of crew-cut grass, brooding and bemoaning, I stopped at some bleachers nearby.

"It's got to be about more than just you," a voice said.

"Yeah, I know. I need to deny myself and serve other people and stop wallowing," I said back to the voice.

"Leeana, it's got to be about more than just you." I heard it again.

I pulled out a small notebook I had with me and wrote down the phrase. *It's got to be about more than just you.* I looked at it long and hard, underlined it a time or two, and then put a big circle around it and added some stars. *It's got to be about more than just you.*

All the focus on my own inadequacies and failings, all the time spent managing and apologizing and fearing, all the self-loathing and shame was all about me. Small, fearful, uninspired me.

If I learned anything in Bahrain, I learned that I am more and deeper, that my voice is richer and stronger and bigger and wilder than I ever imagined. I needed to stop apologizing and start letting the world hear my real, true voice. Not the fitful frettings of a false self, but the deep, soulful voice I know is down there somewhere.

Great power resides in a voice that sings for no audience and searches for no approval, and yet owns the depth and breadth and passion it has been given. Ask Wanida. The Russian-Georgian restaurant hasn't been the same since.

27
dancing

Dancing is, to me, one of the most vulnerable things a person can do. I didn't grow up dancing; I grew up Baptist. The big joke goes something like this: "Why don't Baptists believe in premarital sex? Because it leads to dancing."

I can't dance well, and I'm often embarrassed to try, so I was especially shocked when I recently met a very bookish middle-aged woman (wearing knit pants and sensible shoes) who told me she loves to dance. Come again?

Her? I thought to myself. *She* likes to dance? I just couldn't picture it. She went on to share that she loved dancing on the beach as her act of worship to God.

"It's my favorite thing to do," she says.

I have no idea what to do with this information. So let me get this straight: She dances as her worship? Right there on the beach? Can you imagine? What an insane concept! Wild enough, actually, that I find myself suddenly envious of Plain Jane the Beach Dancer.

I am not this woman, though I desperately long to be. First of all, I long to spend my days in the "spacious place" the psalmist talks about, a place so wide open you can't help but be wild and free. It seems this woman has an internal compass straight toward such places. Second, I'd love to be able to dance in front of the world with her kind of spirit and passion. Third, I love the beach. And if I could dance at all, that's where I'd want to dance too.

I grew up with bad asthma. When I'd have a particularly aggressive attack, my doctor would tell my mom to take me down to the beach. Once there, fresh ocean air replaced our valley smog, and I could breathe again. So we spent a good deal of time at the beach. We'd go to San Elijo in the summer to camp. We'd go to Mission Beach on Christmas Day to walk. We'd visit La Jolla or Coronado to play in the waves. The beach is the place where I have always been able to breathe, to take into my lungs something deeply healing.

About a year after I met Plain Jane the Beach Dancer, I was walking along the shore, and I remembered her. As I looked out on the sea, I pictured her dancing along the edge of the wet sand, her feet swirling through the surf.

That particular day I needed peace from the raging noise of the toxic voices. I was tired, and tension stiffened my shoulders and neck. As I walked, I found a large pile of reeds. I wouldn't normally do what I did next. I laid down right in the middle of the reeds. It struck me, in the moment, as a cathartic thing to do.

Sometimes healing requires things to get worse before they get better. At times, I start to feel invisible, like I'm slipping away from real life. My mind feels preoccupied, my soul is heavy, and my body feels tired. Nestling into nature is a powerful antidote. Letting sand or dirt or grass or water or air touch you reminds you that your skin is there, that you do exist in the world, that you are alive after all.

The reeds were warm, and their scent was saturated with sand, seaweed, and sun. I settled deeper into them and let the

found art

moment happen. My body needed oxygen, so I began taking deep breaths — long, heaving inhalations and exhalations — intentionally forcing the air to move in and out of my lungs. I stretched one arm at a time over my chest and tried to work out the tension. I know I was a strange sight, but in that moment, and for once, I really didn't care.

I thought of myself in Bahrain, standing in front of Capital Centre trying to decide between Mega Mart and the meat market, paralyzed with indecision and fear. I considered it an act of redemptive bravery to lie down in the reeds, something I might never have done if I hadn't already discovered beauty in such foreign places.

As I became one with my nest, I thought of baby Moses floating down the Nile River in his reed basket, and I just laid there breathing. I breathed and breathed and listened and quieted until I almost fell asleep right there in the reeds. I didn't realize how much I was carrying until I became silent, closed my eyes, and began to breathe.

I want to be the Beach Dancer. Really badly, actually. But I want to be the perfect version with envious rhythm and a tight yoga outfit. People who stopped to watch me would be inspired; they'd cry and pray and go on their way, feeling as though they'd seen God.

But God let Plain Jane be the Beach Dancer.

Maybe someday, as I continue to heal from the shame that still revisits me at times, I will be healed enough to walk out to the shoreline and create something beautiful for myself and God without the fear of what others might think. Today, though, I am thankful for my ability to breathe, to be the Reed Breather. I am thankful to have found something beautiful in the reeds — full lungs filled with truth and freedom.

dancing

birthing:
an ending and a beginning

Steve and I have been trying to start a family for some time now. Over a year, actually, which is an important benchmark because twelve months is the amount of time our doctor wants us to try before he will talk about "next steps."

When Steve and I decided we were ready to start a family—at least, when we thought we were ready to take the first steps toward trying to have a family—we moved forward in a non-committed sort of fashion. If it happens, great; if it doesn't happen right away, fine.

I took the *laissez-faire* attitude because such indifference provided a smoke screen for my fear. My fear was twofold: that I would get pregnant, and that I wouldn't. I was afraid of all the change a child would bring to our lives, all the sacrifices and chaos and sleep deprivation. I was also afraid of what would happen if, for some reason, we weren't ever able to experience those glorious interruptions.

As fate would dictate, twelve months (plus or minus) into the endeavor, we were still barren. Our doctor ordered a few routine tests, all of which came back completely normal. *Normal* is both good and bad—good because we were healthy, bad because no one could figure out why I wasn't getting pregnant. The doctor called to talk through our options.

We both agreed the process would have been so much easier if I just—whoops!—tripped and fell and found out I was pregnant. Instead, we got the distinct honor of really having to decide if we wanted a baby and how far we were willing to go to get one. Steve and I felt a bit lost, but we both agreed we were not going to let fear make our decision for us. I felt proud of that conclusion, and we moved forward with the least invasive form of fertility help—a tiny white pill no bigger than a Tic Tac.

Today, I am much like that Leeana who stepped off the plane and into a foreign world. The seasons of my life are changing yet again, and I find myself standing in the numbing gap of experience and integration. I find myself on the edge of the rock preparing to jump, looking at the glossy black-and-white sonogram pictures I've just added to my collage.

At this very moment, I am waiting for two tiny babies—yes, TWO babies—to be born. After a long journey, Steve and I are expecting our first children, twins (thanks to my familial predisposition and that magic Tic Tac). They've been growing big and strong for some time, kicking around in there like two tussling puppies. I'm told they will make their appearance any week now.

I have no idea what to feel or how we'll manage. I find that moving into motherhood is much like moving to the Middle East. I'm unsure. I'm new and inexperienced, yet again. I don't know where I belong in this new culture and new world, and I surely don't speak the language as of yet. Though I know things won't feel this way forever, I'm temporarily aimless and out of sorts, uprooted all over again.

As much as I want to worry and wonder about this stage of my life, I am assured that I've been carried here, just as I was carried to Bahrain. I hope against hope, even trust against trust, that God will meet me in this new land, as he has met me in foreign lands before.

In Arabic, the word *Bahrain* means "two seas." Apparently the country was named Bahrain because of the freshwater springs that are found within the salty seas surrounding the island.

In the briny salt waters of upheaval and incomprehension, fresh and living water swirls and pours. Perhaps the power, the beauty, is in the commingling of the two.

That is the great art of life, a mysterious collage of unexpected elements. Even today, we are putting down our layers, one beside another, creating and recreating ourselves. He is making everything beautiful in its time. While we wait, we must breathe and heal and grieve and become. We don't see the beauty immediately, but as we look back, we find the art in and through it all.

To be continued . . .

acknowledgments

Many people have believed this book into being. Whether they know it or not, they have each protected the vision when I was too tired, too overwhelmed, or too fearful to carry the mantle myself.

And so, I would like to say thank you . . .

to Angela Scheff for five years of faithfulness. Like a good coach, you have expected and required more than I thought I had. For that, the book is better.

to the Zondervan team for investing with excellence and generosity and creativity.

to Dr. William Gribbin for giving me the confidence to push out into the world and for championing me.

to Ash, Stack, Melba, Jilly, Tush, and Suz. *Teammates* doesn't even begin to describe it. You each in your own way predicted this was possible before I ever had a glimpse. I will never forget the way we laughed.

to Coach Chris Phillips for helping to make me strong — body and mind.

to Paul Joiner for reminding me every day for three years of the great power of creativity.

to Karen Cooper for helping me find my way through some dark days, only to discover the light was there all along.

to Elaine Hamilton for encouraging me to be wild and brave, for holding my hand week after week at The Living Room, and for reading with such great sensitivity and support.

to Amie for collecting a steady stream of affirmations to keep me going and for always letting me walk into your office.

to Rebes and Katie G and Eric J for your ever-faithful interest and enthusiasm.

to Corrie for reading over a year's worth of drafts, for the narrative arc and other good questions, and for one quote after another that made me feel sane and understood.

to Jamie for the thousand little ways you befriend me that always seem to add up to a huge, immeasurable gift. Thank you for your consistency.

to the Round Table families — the Andersons, Eatons, Hammetts, Hearns, Van Proyens, and Wildeys. More than friends, you are life companions.

to Daddy and Becky for your tireless care of me and mine. Your abundant and reliable servanthood has humbled me and made the dailyness of life possible. Thank you for the great gift of your availability.

to JT and BT. Little did I know that when I found Steve, I also found two more faithful warriors. I see where he gets it. Thank you for praying, giving, advising, traveling, investing, and loving so deeply.

to Loach and Trey Boy (and Lance and Elyse). You are my people. Where you go, I will go. I love you fiercely and without limit, just as you have loved me.

to Peter and Jacquline for being great defenders and creators of art. I hope you are inspired by these pages.

to Linsey for keeping the tune when I couldn't hear the music, for harmonizing when the melody had gone flat in my head, for adding scores and anthems and arias and hymns of great beauty to my life. And, for believing that it all matters. Keep singing.

to Tina. I remember a time when we were sitting on a lifeguard tower watching the sunset, eating cheeseburgers, and swapping stories. How much and how little things have changed. Thank you for listening to my life for the last twenty-one years, and for your strength.

to Pastor Matt Hammett, the entire Flood Staff (especially JP, Scottillo, Lins, AK, Amie, Noel, Eric, and Minders), and the Flood community Steve and I are so grateful to call home. Thank you for letting me go. You have been generous beyond measure.

to my GG girls — Pirate Debs, Burrit, Joje, Wanstrauss, Corrith, KJ, and Tates. You have kept me buoyed when I thought I would sink for sure. Seeing your faces around the table and your names in my in-box every week was and is the most practical love. Thank you for showing up. I am utterly and entirely indebted.

to Luke Stephen and Lane Watkins. You have been my closest companions through this journey, keeping me quiet (and then not-so-quiet) company while I wrote. Mommy loves you.

to Steve for sleeping on the couch while I wrote in the living room that one night so I didn't have to feel alone in my anxiety, for throwing that amazing surprise party to celebrate the contract (I'll never forget Matt and Seth hauling in the writing desk), for talking me off the ledge each and every time I was convinced the gig was up, for one pot of coffee after another, for scraping me up off the floor, for coming to me. And, of course, for Bahrain. You are my best friend.

to Moach, my inimitable mother — matchless in almost every conceivable sense. I hope you aren't too terribly mortified! Though we are both great lovers of words, they sometimes fail. Now is one of those times. What language can I borrow to say thanks? There is none worthy. So I will say it by living and writing and creating and believing, as I know such endeavors are a reflection of all things you have taught me to love.

Also, thank you to Maya, who graciously allowed me to tell her story in the telling of my own.

definition of terms

Abaya—"Cloak" in Arabic; an overgarment worn by some women in parts of the Islamic world. Traditional abayas are black and may be either a large square of fabric draped from the shoulders or head or a long caftan. The *abaya* covers the whole body except for the face, feet, and hands.

Corniche—A waterfront promenade usually paralleled by a main road.

Dhow—A traditional Arab sailing vessel with one or more lateen sails primarily used along the coasts of the Arabian Peninsula, Pakistan, India, and East Africa.

Dinar—The name of the official currency (paper money) in Bahrain.

Fils—A subdivision of currency (coins) in Bahrain. One Bahraini *dinar* is equivalent to 1,000 *fils*. Also used to refer to a small amount of money in general.

Imam—An Islamic leadership position, often the leader of a mosque and the community, who leads the prayer during Islamic gatherings.

Insha'Allah—An Arabic term meaning "God willing," or "If God wills it."

Minaret—"Lighthouse" in Arabic. The tower attached to a mosque, it has distinctive architectural features such as tall spires with onion-shaped crowns, usually either free standing or much taller than any surrounding support structure.

Mosque—A place of prayer and worship for followers of Islam.

Muezzin—A chosen person at the mosque who leads the call (*adhan*) to Friday service and the five daily prayers (also known as the *salat*) from one of the mosque's minarets. (In most modern mosques, electronic amplification aids the muezzins.) The professional muezzin is chosen to serve at the mosque for his good character, voice, and skills; however, he is not considered a cleric but is comparable to a Christian sexton. When calling to prayer, the muezzin faces the *qiblah* (direction of the *Kaaba*, the central sanctuary, in Mecca) while he cries out the *adhan*. The acts of the muezzin are considered an art form, reflected in the melodious chanting of the *adhan*.

Mumtaz—A brand of premium gasoline sold in Bahrain; an Arabic term meaning "the best," used to describe a "premium" brand of gasoline.

Naan—Round flatbread made of flour.

Qur'an—Islamic holy book.

Sharia—The holy law of God in Islam.

Shi'a—The second largest denomination of Islam, after Sunni Islam. Similar to other branches of Islam, Shi'a Islam is based on the teachings of the Islamic holy book, the Qur'an, and the message of the final prophet of Islam, Muhammad. In contrast to other branches, Shi'a Islam holds that Muhammad's family, the *Ahl al-Bayt* ("People of the House"), and certain individuals among his descendants, known as *Imams*, have special spiritual and political rule over the community. Shi'a Muslims also believe that Ali, Muhammad's cousin and son-in-law, was the first of these *Imams* and was the rightful successor to Muhammad and thus reject the legitimacy of the first three Rashidun caliphs. Shi'a Muslims, though a minority in the Muslim world, constitute the majority of the populations in Iran, Azerbaijan, Bahrain, and Iraq.

Shukran—An Arabic expression meaning "thank you."

Souq—A commercial quarter in an Arab city. The term is often used to designate the market in any Arabized or Muslim city. It may also refer to the weekly market in some smaller towns, where neutrality from tribal conflicts would be declared to permit the exchange of surplus goods. In Modern Standard Arabic, *souq* refers to markets in both the physical sense and the abstract economic sense.

Sunni—The largest denomination of Islam. Sunni Islam is also referred to as Ahl as-Sunnah wa'l-Jamâ'ah ("people of the example [of Muhammad] and the community"). The word *Sunni* comes from *Sunnah*, which means "the words and actions or example of the Islamic prophet Muhammad."

Thobe—An ankle-length garment, usually with long sleeves, similar to a robe. Typically worn by men in the Arabian Peninsula and some surrounding countries. Normally made of cotton, but heavier materials such as sheep's wool can also be used, especially in colder climates.

discussion prompts

intended for personal or group reflection

my collage: an introduction

"What if God were taking all of my life—the glorious and the gutless, the griefs and the gains—and piecing each bit together like a collage so that when finished, something extraordinary would emerge?" (12)

"That's the thing about these journeys into foreign places. They have a way of making us different if we will let them. We can resist the beauty that is waiting for us, but if we will enter the frightening place—if we will engage ourselves in the context of this new culture—we will see that there was no shortcut to transformation" (13).

- Read Ecclesiastes 3:1–8. Which of the twenty-eight "seasons" particularly resonates with you today? Why?

1: uprooting

"Loss is the little sister who always tags along with change" (20).

- Share about a time when you experienced a dramatic change in your life. How did loss accompany that change?

- When I feel out of place, I . . .

- How is your soul today?

2: loving

"Truly letting someone in entirely and enduring their desire to love you, knowing they will love so imperfectly, is really very difficult" (27).

- Share about a time when someone you cared about let you down, hurt you, betrayed you, or rejected you. It may have been an overt offense against you, or perhaps something subtle — even unintentional — that has stayed with you for a long time. How has that relational rift affected your ability to trust others? To receive love from others?

- What fears do you have when you think about or experience intimacy? (For example, that the other person will see your flaws and not want to be close to you, that the other person will hurt you, that too much will be expected of you, that you won't live up to their expectations.)

3: holding on

"A few things are worth holding on to no matter what is required—a dream, a relationship, faith. The hard part is, sometimes you can't see or touch or feel the dream, or the person, or God, and you have to believe anyway" (36).

- Share about a time when you had to hold on to something important to you. What was it like to have to fight for the thing you believed in?

- Have you ever sabotaged a dream or a relationship or your faith because you were afraid of what it would take to hold on to it? Share about that experience.

- Sometimes holding on is about believing and enduring. Is there a situation in your life today that is requiring extraordinary belief and endurance? What do you need in order to help you hold on?

4: war

"I am the kind of person who, at any moment, is anxiously overcompensating for strange insecurities such as . . ." (42).

—

"The war I'm fighting is the epic battle of myself against myself—a bruising, losing sort of war (as all war is) that I can't seem to shake loose from" (43).

- What are some strange insecurities you overcompensate for?

- Share some of the toxic messages that you hear.

- Being brave means . . .

5: quit searching

"I'd spent large amounts of time on a search for something—love, worth, affirmation, acceptance—only to discover that I'd been searching in all the wrong places. My own efforts left me circling, looking for life on my own terms, when what I really needed to do was quit searching for a loophole or an exception or my own way" (50–51).

• Share about a relationship you've had that was unsafe. Were you the unsafe person or did you attach yourself to someone who was unsafe?

• Sometimes we look to another person to provide things they can't ultimately provide for us—validation of our worth or identity, for example. Have you ever gone searching for such affirmations in the wrong places? Share about that experience.

• I feel safe with someone else when ...

6: keeping silence

"I've made a habit out of filling up most every quiet moment with at least a little bit of noise—enough to keep me distracted from the discomfort of not really knowing myself" (54).

"The risk of sitting in the silence, as we all know, is what we will find there" (56).

• When was the last time you experienced stillness and silence? Do you tend to seek out quiet or are you more likely to resist it?

- If I could spend an afternoon doing anything, I would ...

- Are you a person who tends to hide behind achieving, striving, going, doing? What drives you?

7: healing

"Beauty possesses great power to heal" (63).

"The beauty of the world was lost on me, and all the things I loved were forgotten in lieu of all the things I thought I needed to be" (64).

- Make two columns on a piece of paper. At the top of the first column write "I AM." At the top of the other column write "I AM NOT." Make a list under each of who you are and who you are not. For example, I AM creative. I AM great at throwing parties. I AM making progress. I AM NOT who my boss says I am. I AM NOT my sister. I AM NOT going to live in fear anymore. Share what you wrote with your group or with someone you trust.

- Share about a place that has been healing to you.

- I am inspired by ...

8: gathering

"Somehow, in Bahrain, I rediscovered the nerve to believe that my truest self mattered, that my thoughts counted, that art for art's sake was indeed a valid use of my time — whether or not things came out perfectly" (72).

- Share about an area of your life where you have wanted to appear perfect. What has that pursuit of perfection cost you?

- If you could do anything with your life, what would you do? What keeps you from doing it?

- Who were you at age nine? What was important to you then? How did you spend your time? What were your fears? Answer the same questions about yourself at age thirteen, eighteen, twenty-one, thirty, forty, and so on. How are you still similar to yourself at those ages? How are you different?

9: building up

"We focused on assets instead of always belaboring liabilities" (78).

"Bodybuilding takes much more courage than body hating" (78).

- Are you more likely to focus on your assets or on your liabilities? Which are you more likely to focus on in others?

- It takes courage for me to accept myself because ...

- Share something about yourself you really like. Share something about someone else you really like. Which one was more difficult? Why?

10: laughing

"Rare and sacred are the moments when the most organic gift appears—though it may leave as quickly as it comes—that interrupts the darkness all around it. The world may be falling apart, may be at war even, but the sound of laughter can be heard from one small corner as it spills out and fills in the deepest grooves of sadness" (87).

- Who is someone you laugh with? How has your laughter with that person been life-giving?

- Share about an area of your life where you may need to lighten up a bit. Is there a situation you are currently taking too seriously? Are you taking yourself too seriously?

- I find joy in ...

11: tearing

"Pain is gawky and ungainly and never ties up neatly. It hangs on like an old infirm dog that needs to be put down. For all these reasons, I hate sitting in the discomfort. I hate the way hurting makes me feel out of control and weak" (96).

- How does being in pain make you feel? Do you tend to avoid feeling pain? Does pain feel like weakness to you?

- How do you feel about conflict? Do you tend to be overly avoidant or overly combatant?

- Share about a recent conflict you handled poorly.

- I feel defensive when ...

12: mending

"Putting things back together is never easy; that's why mending is such a sacred act" (102).

* Share about a tear in your life that has been difficult to mend.

* I am having trouble forgiving _____ because ...

13: letting go

"There are some things that happen in life that are difficult. And, as if you were setting a boat out to sea, you have to take those things and let them go, let them float out and away. And only God can help us do that" (109).

"All we have to do is remain the slightest bit open to becoming well" (110).

* Read John 5:1 – 15. When it comes to healing, we have a part and God has a part. What is our part and what is his?

* Getting well means ...

* Share about something in your life that you are holding on to that it's time to let go of. What do you need in order to let it go?

14: searching

"No one ever had to live lost again" (117).

"I, too—in my own way and in my own space and in my own time—was on a pilgrimage to worship the Christ child" (118).

- Where are you in your spiritual seeking today? Actively pursuing, privately interested, apathetic, burned-out, doubting, turned off, tired, bitter from the past, disillusioned, curious, confused, numb, cautiously open?

- I feel lost when ...

- I am waiting for God to ...

15: embracing

"I often wonder where God is, what he's up to, how he's moving, when his plan will unfold.... So often, though, he seems out of reach, his voice is hard to hear, and his plan feels foggy" (123–24).

- I feel close to God when ...

- I feel far from God when ...

- Share about a time when you were trying to discern God's plan but it wasn't clear.

- Choose three words to describe God. Why did you choose those words?

16: dying

"Desire, as we all know, is the most scandalous freedom there is" (131).

- I truly desire ...

- Share about something you really desired but didn't get. How did that disappointment affect you? Your relationship with God? Your ability to be honest about your true desires?

- Do you experience desire toward God?

17: scattering

"If I were better—if I were one of the good people—I would feel as though I were walking hand in hand with God during every moment of every day" (133).

—

"It wasn't all up to me" (136).

- Do you ever feel as though God is closer to other people than he is to you? Why do you feel that way?

- When you think about God, are you more likely to feel unconditionally loved or consistently inadequate?

- It is difficult for me to admit I need God because ...

18: peace

"It's strange how life often requires something foreign to connect us with something that, in the end, was so close all along. Sometimes we need a change of scenery in order to see what is really there inside us—all the parts and pieces of ourselves that have somehow been lost but are in desperate need of finding again" (143–44).

- Share about a time in life when you experienced a "foreign place"—a season of life that felt uncomfortable and unfamiliar. How did that place change you?

- Do you need peace in your life right now? Share about any turmoil you are experiencing.

- Peace is . . .

19: killing

"The risk killed fear's power, and I was—for one brief second—brave" (148).

"The voices of fear began clamoring once again, and I knew the only way to silence them was to step out into the very thing I wanted to avoid" (150).

- Name a risk you need to take. What is keeping you from taking it?

- I am afraid of . . .

- Share about a time when you were brave.

20: weeping

"Coming back from somewhere significant—a pilgrimage of any kind—is personal, particular, and often lonely" (153).

- Share about a time when you had to reenter "real life" after a particularly profound experience.

- I am trying to say good-bye to ...

21: planting

"Even in the most desperate places, even in the most desolate deserts, even in the most foreign of soils, something beautiful can and will grow" (157).

- Draw yourself as a tree. What do your leaves, trunk, and branches look like? What season are you in? What animals and other life are present? Share your tree with your group or someone you trust.

- Do you feel more planted or more uprooted today? Explain.

found art

22: mourning

"Pain, like no other place perhaps, is where our art is born, where our stories are written, our canvases brushed, our scores composed. Though we so often want to deny the discomfort, suffering is one of the few things that can lead us to the place where we find the God we so desperately long for" (166–67).

"Yes, even though we walk through the valley of the shadow of death, he is with us. In our greatest need, he sees us" (167).

- The most difficult thing I have ever had to grieve is …

- Today I am grieving …

23: hating

"I hate that the world is cruel, and I hate that I feel powerless against the brutality" (171).

- Share about a time when you were angry with God.

- I hate …

24: breaking down

"I felt the warm presence of my community. My community. Imperfect strangers—who are all a little crazy, might I add—standing together to worship and be healed, shoulder to shoulder and foot to foot" (180).

* Really letting other people in to my life is difficult because they might . . .

* Really letting other people in to my life is difficult because I might . . .

* Share about a time when you felt lonely.

25: turning away

"I longed to turn away from the lies, but the truth was hard to believe" (183).

* One lie I want to stop believing about myself is . . .

* I feel fake when . . .

26: speaking

"All the focus on my own inadequacies and failings, all the time spent managing and apologizing and fearing, all the self-loathing and shame was all about me. Small, fearful, uninspired me" (187).

- Share an area of your life where you experience shame (a sense of being flawed).

- How are people-pleasing, perfectionism, significance chasing, self-promotion, or a need for approval manifested in your life? Are these common experiences or just something you feel once in awhile? Are there specific people or circumstances that trigger any or all of these?

- One step I can take toward wholeness and healing is ...

27: dancing

"I long to spend my days in the 'spacious place' the psalmist talks about, a place so wide open you can't help but be wild and free" (189).

- I'm in a spacious place when ...

- True freedom is ...

- Share about a time in your life when you felt really alive.

afterword:
birthing: an ending and a beginning

"That is the great art of life, a mysterious collage of unexpected elements. Even today, we are putting down our layers, one beside another, creating and recreating ourselves. He is making everything beautiful in its time. While we wait, we must breathe and heal and grieve and become. We don't see the beauty immediately, but as we look back, we find the art in and through it all" (195).

• Create a collage of your life. Use words and pictures from magazines, odds and ends from around your house, and original paintings or drawings or writings. Don't worry about creating something perfect. Just be true to yourself and choose items that particularly resonate with you, even if you don't know exactly why.

Share your collage with your group or with someone you trust, explaining each item's significance to you.

About the Author

A native of San Diego, California, Leeana Tankersley received her Bachelor of Arts degree in English from Liberty University and her Master of Arts degree in English from West Virginia University. After marrying her husband, Steve, Leeana lived in the Middle East during the Iraq war and then returned to San Diego to work at Flood Church. She and Steve and their twins, Luke and Lane, live in Coronado, California. Follow Leeana at *www.gypsyink.com.*

Share Your Thoughts

With the Author: Your comments will be forwarded to the author when you send them to *zauthor@zondervan.com*.

With Zondervan: Submit your review of this book by writing to *zreview@zondervan.com*.

Free Online Resources at
www.zondervan.com

Zondervan AuthorTracker: Be notified whenever your favorite authors publish new books, go on tour, or post an update about what's happening in their lives.

Daily Bible Verses and Devotions: Enrich your life with daily Bible verses or devotions that help you start every morning focused on God.

Free Email Publications: Sign up for newsletters on fiction, Christian living, church ministry, parenting, and more.

Zondervan Bible Search: Find and compare Bible passages in a variety of translations at www.zondervanbiblesearch.com.

Other Benefits: Register yourself to receive online benefits like coupons and special offers, or to participate in research.